THE RIME OF THE
ANCIENT MARINER
AND OTHER POEMS OF THE ROMANTIC ERA

Selections by Coleridge, Blake,
Wordsworth, Byron, Shelley, Keats

Prestwick House

LITERARY TOUCHSTONE CLASSICS™

P.O. Box 658 Clayton, Delaware 19938 • www.prestwickhouse.com

Senior Editor: Paul Moliken

Editors: Douglas Grudzina and Lisa M. Miller

Cover Design: Kelly Valentine Vasami/Larry Knox

Production: Jerry Clark

Prestwick House
LITERARY TOUCHSTONE CLASSICS™

P.O. Box 658 • Clayton, Delaware 19938
Tel: 1.800.932.4593
Fax: 1.888.718.9333
Web: www.prestwickhouse.com

Prestwick House Teaching Units™, Activity Packs™, and Response Journals™ are the perfect complement for these editions. To purchase teaching resources for this book, visit www.prestwickhouse.com

This Prestwick House edition is an unabridged republication, with minor emendations, of these Romantic poems, taken from various sources in the public domain.

ISBN: 978-1-58049-171-6

THE RIME OF THE ANCIENT MARINER

AND OTHER POEMS OF THE ROMANTIC ERA

CONTENTS

Notes

What is a literary classic and why are these classic works important to the world?

A literary classic is a work of the highest excellence that has something important to say about life and/or the human condition and says it with great artistry. A classic, through its enduring presence, has withstood the test of time and is not bound by time, place, or customs. It speaks to us today as forcefully as it spoke to people one hundred or more years ago, and as forcefully as it will speak to people of future generations. For this reason, a classic is said to have universality.

The 18th century was a time of revolution; the French Revolution, especially, was supposed to usher in a new era of enlightenment, brotherhood, and individual freedom. The artistic movement that arose in Europe in reaction to  the events of this time is called Romanticism, and it is characterized by a stressing of emotion and imagination, as opposed to the emphasis on classical forms that was important to previous artists. In England, the major Romantic poets were Samuel Taylor Coleridge, William Blake, Percy Bysshe Shelley, Lord Byron, William Wordsworth, and John Keats. These poets took up the revolutionary ideas of personal and spiritual emancipation through language that is often bold and simple, like the speech of the common people of England.

Romantic poetry frequently focuses on images of nature, which is viewed as a force that expresses sympathy with human beings. Romanticism also features supernatural events and includes melancholy settings, such as deserted castles or monasteries on lonely hillsides.

A concern for human society also marks the early English Romantics. Blake describes a time when Albion (England) will be free from oppression and injustice, and all men will enter into a new age and a new heaven on Earth. Wordsworth despises the ugliness of the expanding cities and urges a return to a spiritual home in nature. Later Romantic poets, though, especially Keats, focus more on the intense emotions and deep paradoxes of human existence.

Despite the variety of opinion and style within English Romantic poetry, one idea remains central to the movement: Individual experience is the primary source of truth and knowledge. In fact, some recent scholars have attributed the modern ideas of personality to the Romantic poets, whose focus on personal, emotional, and subjective experience may have given rise to our notions of individuality.

Reading Pointers for Sharper Insights

The Romantic Movement was a literary, artistic, and intellectual movement in the late 18th and early 19th centuries. It began as a reaction against the rigid conventions—artistic, social, and political—of the Enlightenment and asserted the power and the value of the individual.

Romanticism stressed strong emotion and the individual imagination as the ultimate critical and moral authority. The Romantic poets, therefore, felt free to challenge traditional notions of *form*. They likewise found themselves abandoning social conventions, particularly the privileges of the aristocracy, which they believed to be detrimental to individual fulfillment.

Because Romanticism is, at its core, a rebellion *against* rigid standards of form, taste, and behavior, it is difficult to establish a set of standards to *define* Romanticism. It is possible, however, to point out some common motifs that offer an overview of what the Romantic poets believed and tried to accomplish in their poetry.

The Politics of the Romantics:

- The Romantics were, for the most part, disheartened liberals.

- The successful revolution of the American colonies against the oppressive British crown and the developing revolution in France were exciting to the Romantics.

- Blake, Wordsworth, Byron, and Shelley all lost heart, however, because of the Reign of Terror in France and the rise of Napoleon as the French Emperor.

- The Romantic focus on the imagination was a direct response to 18th-century rationalism.

The Psychology of the Romantics:

- The nature of experience: its duality and fleeting quality were of great interest to the Romantics. Notice Blake's contrast between Innocence and Experience, the role of memory in Wordsworth's work, Shelley's lamenting the passing of an experience, and Keats's assertion that the *imagined* experience is better than the actual, in that it will never end.

- Beauty was to be found in Nature, not in man-made objects or concepts.

- The Romantics sought solitude in Nature, believing that the key to all emotional healing could be found there.

- Nature imagery is the most predominant feature of Romantic literature.

- The concept of a pantheistic Nature (God exists in all things) became almost a religion for Wordsworth, Shelley, and Keats.

- In the "religion" of the Romantics, virtue was exemplified by being true to one's nature while "sin" occurred when denying one's own nature or forcing someone else to conform to a foreign code of principles or behavior. (In *The Marriage of Heaven and Hell,* Blake wrote: "One law for the Lion and Ox is oppression.")

The Romantic Sense of Beauty:

- While the literature of the Enlightenment focused on the hero and the high-ranking socialite, the Romantics celebrated the commoner, the laborer, and the "underprivileged."

- 18th-century esthetics had favored the highly ornate and artificial (as epitomized by Baroque music and architecture), but the Romantics strove to emphasize beauty in simplicity and plainness.

The Byronic Hero:

Taking into consideration the personal traits the Romantics found most admirable—passionate conviction, absolute individualism and independence, a disregard for restrictive authority and the outmoded or unjust laws it represents—it follows that the Romantic notion of the hero would be just such a person. Byron's most famous characters, *Manfred, Childe Harold,* and *Don Juan,* typify this type of hero, as did Byron himself. Thus, the Romantic hero came to be known as the Byronic Hero.

SAMUEL TAYLOR COLERIDGE

"What if you slept, and what if in your sleep you dreamed, and what if in your dreams you went to heaven and there you plucked a strange and beautiful flower, and what if when you awoke you had the flower in your hand? Ah, what then?"

—SAMUEL TAYLOR COLERIDGE,
Biographia Literaria

SAMUEL TAYLOR COLERIDGE was born October 21, 1772, the son of a vicar. When Coleridge was nine, his father died, and his mother sent him away to boarding school, often not allowing him to return home for holidays and vacations. As an adult, Coleridge would idealize his father, but his relationship with his mother would always be strained.

He attended Jesus College at Cambridge University, but never completed a degree, one time leaving school to join the military to escape a woman who had rejected him. While at university, Coleridge became friends with Robert Southey, and the two developed plans to establish a utopian commune in Pennsylvania. Coleridge and Southey married sisters Edith and Sarah Fricker, but Coleridge's marriage was never truly happy.

In 1793, Coleridge met and became instant friends with William Wordsworth. With Wordsworth, he wrote and published *Lyrical Ballads*. While Wordsworth contributed a greater *number* of poems to the work,

Coleridge's *The Rime of the Ancient Mariner* received the most attention.

Throughout their friendship and careers, Wordsworth would always be the more productive poet, while Coleridge's work would gain the notice of critics and readers.

Coleridge allegedly suffered from a number of physical ailments, including facial neuralgia, and in 1796, he started using opium as a pain reliever. He would become addicted to the narcotic, and this would eventually affect his career as a poet and his friendship with Wordsworth.

His intensifying opium addiction, an unhappy marriage, and a growing estrangement from Wordsworth all contributed to a period of depression, which included a severe lack of confidence in his own poetic ability. He gradually spent more and more time alone, studying philosophy and traveling the Continent. Although considered by many to be a "giant among dwarfs," Coleridge never quite regained his confidence.

In 1816, his addiction worsening, his spirits depressed, and his family alienated, Coleridge took up residence in Highgate, the home of physician James Gillman. Here he finished his major prose work, the *Biographia Literaria*, twenty-five chapters of autobiographical notes and discussions on various subjects, including literary theory and criticism.

Coleridge died of heart failure in Highgate on July 25, 1834.

The Rime of the Ancient Mariner in Seven Parts

From *Lyrical Ballads*[†]

Facile credo, plures esse Naturas invisibiles quam visibiles in rerum universitate. Sed horum omnium familiam quis nobis enarrabit? et gradus et cognationes et discrimina et singulorum munera? Quid agunt? quae loca habitant? Harum rerum notitiam semper ambivit ingenium humanum, nunquam attigit. Juvat, interea, non diffiteor, quandoque in animo, tanquam in tabulâ, majoris et melioris mundi imaginem contemplari: ne mens assuefacta hodiernae vitae minutiis se contrahat nimis, et tota subsidat in pusillas cogitationes. Sed veritati interea invigilandum est, modusque servandus, ut certa ab incertis, diem a nocte, distinguamus. – T. Burnet, *Archaeol. Phil.*, p. 68[†]

ARGUMENT

How a Ship having passed the Line[†] was driven by Storms to the cold Country towards the South Pole; and how from thence she made her course to the tropical Latitude of the Great Pacific Ocean; and of the strange things that befell; and in what manner the Ancyent Marinere came back to his own Country.

PART THE FIRST.

It is an ancient Mariner,
And he stoppeth one of three.
"By thy long grey beard and glittering eye,
Now wherefore stoppest thou me?

An ancient Mariner meeteth three gallants bidden to a wedding feast, and detaineth one.

5 "The Bridegroom's doors are opened wide,
And I am next of kin;
The guests are met, the feast is set:
May'st hear the merry din."

[†]Terms marked in the text with (†) can be looked up in the Glossary for additional information.

He holds him with his skinny hand,
10 "There was a ship," quoth he.
"Hold off! unhand me, grey-beard loon!"
Eftsoons his hand dropt he.

The Wedding-Guest is
spell-bound by the eye
of the old seafaring
man, and constrained
to hear his tale.

He holds him with his glittering eye—
The Wedding-Guest stood still,
15 And listens like a three years child:
The Mariner hath his will.

The Wedding-Guest sat on a stone:
He cannot choose but hear;
And thus spake on that ancient man,
20 The bright-eyed Mariner.

The ship was cheered, the harbour cleared,
Merrily did we drop
Below the kirk, below the hill,
Below the light-house top.

The Mariner tells how
the ship sailed south-
ward with a good wind
and fair weather, till it
reached the Line.

25 The Sun came up upon the left,
Out of the sea came he!
And he shone bright, and on the right
Went down into the sea.

Higher and higher every day,
30 Till over the mast at noon†—
The Wedding-Guest here beat his breast,
For he heard the loud bassoon.

The Wedding-
Guest heareth the
bridal music; but the
Mariner continueth
his tale.

The bride hath paced into the hall,
Red as a rose is she;
35 Nodding their heads before her goes
The merry minstrelsy.

The Wedding-Guest he beat his breast,
Yet he cannot choose but hear;
And thus spake on that ancient man,
40 The bright-eyed Mariner.

And now the STORM-BLAST came, and he
Was tyrannous and strong:
He struck with his o'ertaking wings,
And chased south along.

The ship drawn by a storm toward the South Pole.

45 With sloping masts and dipping prow,
As who pursued with yell and blow
Still treads the shadow of his foe
And forward bends his head,
The ship drove fast, loud roared the blast,
50 And southward aye we fled.

And now there came both mist and snow,
And it grew wondrous cold:
And ice, mast-high, came floating by,
As green as emerald.

55 And through the drifts the snowy clifts
Did send a dismal sheen:
Nor shapes of men nor beasts we ken—
The ice was all between.

The land of ice, and of fearful sounds, where no living thing was to be seen.

The ice was here, the ice was there,
60 The ice was all around:
It cracked and growled, and roared and howled,
Like noises in a swound!

At length did cross an Albatross:†
Thorough the fog it came;
65 As if it had been a Christian soul,
We hailed it in God's name.

Till a great sea-bird, called the Albatross, came through the snow-fog, and was received with great joy and hospitality.

It ate the food it ne'er had eat,
And round and round it flew.
The ice did split with a thunder-fit;
70 The helmsman steered us through!

And a good south wind sprung up behind;
The Albatross did follow,
And every day, for food or play,
Came to the mariners' hollo!

And lo! the Albatross proveth a bird of good omen, and followeth the ship as it returned northward through fog and floating ice.

75 In mist or cloud, on mast or shroud,
It perched for vespers nine;†
Whiles all the night, through fog-smoke white,
Glimmered the white Moon-shine.

The ancient Mariner inhospitably killeth the pious bird of good omen.

"God save thee, ancient Mariner!
80 From the fiends, that plague thee thus!—
Why look'st thou so?"—With my cross-bow
I shot the Albatross.

PART THE SECOND.

The Sun now rose upon the right:
Out of the sea came he,
85 Still hid in mist, and on the left
Went down into the sea.

And the good south wind still blew behind
But no sweet bird did follow,
Nor any day for food or play
90 Came to the mariners' hollo!

His shipmates cry out against the ancient Mariner for killing the bird of good luck.

And I had done an hellish thing,
And it would work 'em woe:
For all averred, I had killed the bird
That made the breeze to blow.

But when the fog cleared off, they justify the same, and thus make themselves accomplices in the crime.

95 Nor dim nor red, like God's own head,
The glorious Sun uprist:
Then all averred, I had killed the bird
That brought the fog and mist.
'Twas right, said they, such birds to slay,
100 That bring the fog and mist.

The fair breeze continues; the ship enters the Pacific Ocean, and sails northward, even till it reaches the Line.

The fair breeze blew, the white foam flew,
The furrow followed free:
We were the first that ever burst
Into that silent sea.

105 Down dropt the breeze, the sails dropt down,
     'Twas sad as sad could be;
     And we did speak only to break
     The silence of the sea!

The ship hath been suddenly becalmed.

     All in a hot and copper sky,
110 The bloody Sun, at noon,
     Right up above the mast did stand,
     No bigger than the Moon.

     Day after day, day after day,
     We stuck, nor breath nor motion;
115 As idle as a painted ship
     Upon a painted ocean.†

     Water, water, every where,
     And all the boards did shrink;
     Water, water, every where,
120 Nor any drop to drink.

And the Albatross begins to be avenged.

     The very deep did rot: O Christ!
     That ever this should be!
     Yea, slimy things did crawl with legs
     Upon the slimy sea.

125 About, about, in reel and rout
     The death-fires danced at night;
     The water, like a witch's oils,
     Burnt green and blue and white.

     And some in dreams assured were
130 Of the spirit that plagued us so:
     Nine fathom deep he had followed us
     From the land of mist and snow.†

A Spirit had followed them; one of the invisible inhabitants of this planet, neither departed souls nor angels; concerning whom the learned Jew, Josephus, and the Platonic Constantinopolitan, Michael Psellus, may be consulted. They are very numerous, and there is no climate or element without one or more.

     And every tongue, through utter drought,
     Was withered at the root;
135 We could not speak, no more than if
     We had been choked with soot.

The shipmates in their sore distress, would fain throw the whole guilt on the ancient Mariner: in sign whereof they hang the dead sea-bird round his neck.

Ah! well a-day! what evil looks
Had I from old and young!
Instead of the Cross, the Albatross
140   About my neck was hung.[†]

PART THE THIRD.

There passed a weary time. Each throat
Was parched, and glazed each eye.
A weary time! a weary time!

The ancient Mariner beholdeth a sign in the element afar off.

How glazed each weary eye,
145   When looking westward, I beheld
A something in the sky.

At first it seemed a little speck,
And then it seemed a mist:
It moved and moved, and took at last
150   A certain shape, I wist.

A speck, a mist, a shape, I wist!
And still it neared and neared;
As if it dodged a water-sprite,
It plunged and tacked and veered.

At its nearer approach, it seemeth him to be a ship; and at a dear ransom he freeth his speech from the bonds of thirst.

155   With throats unslaked, with black lips baked,
We could not laugh nor wail;
Through utter drought all dumb we stood!
I bit my arm, I sucked the blood,
And cried, A sail! a sail![†]

160   With throats unslaked, with black lips baked,
Agape they heard me call:

A flash of joy;

Gramercy! they for joy did grin,
And all at once their breath drew in,
As they were drinking all.

And horror follows. For can it be a ship that comes onward without wind or tide?

165   See! see! (I cried) she tacks no more!
Hither to work us weal;
Without a breeze, without a tide,
She steadies with upright keel!

The western wave was all a-flame
170　The day was well nigh done!
　　Almost upon the western wave
　　Rested the broad bright Sun;
　　When that strange shape drove suddenly
　　Betwixt us and the Sun.

175　And straight the Sun was flecked with bars,
　　(Heaven's Mother send us grace!)
　　As if through a dungeon-grate he peered,
　　With broad and burning face.†

It seemeth him but the
skeleton of a ship.

　　Alas! (thought I, and my heart beat loud)
180　How fast she nears and nears!
　　Are those her sails that glance in the Sun,
　　Like restless gossameres!†

　　Are those *her* ribs through which the Sun
　　Did peer, as through a grate?
185　And is that Woman all her crew?
　　Is that a DEATH? and are there two?
　　Is DEATH that woman's mate?

And its ribs are seen
as bars on the face of
the setting Sun. The
Spectre-Woman and
her Death-mate, and
no other on board the
skeleton ship. Like ves-
sel, like crew!

　　Her lips† were red, her looks were free,
　　Her locks were yellow as gold:
190　Her skin was as white as leprosy,
　　The Night-Mare LIFE-IN-DEATH was she,
　　Who thicks man's blood with cold.

　　The naked hulk† alongside came,
　　And the twain were casting dice;†
195　"The game is done! I've won! I've won!"
　　Quoth she, and whistles thrice.†

Death and Life-in-
Death have diced for
the ship's crew, and she
(the latter) winneth
the ancient Mariner.

　　The Sun's rim dips; the stars rush out:
　　At one stride comes the dark;
　　With far-heard whisper, o'er the sea.
200　Off shot the spectre-bark.

No twilight within the
courts of the Sun.

We listened and looked sideways up!
Fear at my heart, as at a cup,
My life-blood seemed to sip!
The stars were dim, and thick the night,

205 The steersman's face by his lamp gleamed white;

At the rising of the Moon,

From the sails the dew did drip—
Till clombe above the eastern bar
The hornéd Moon, with one bright star
Within the nether tip.

One after another,   210   One after one, by the star-dogged Moon
Too quick for groan or sigh,
Each turned his face with a ghastly pang,
And cursed me with his eye.

His shipmates drop down dead.

Four times fifty living men,
215   (And I heard nor sigh nor groan)
With heavy thump, a lifeless lump,
They dropped down one by one.†

But Life-in-Death begins her work on the ancient Mariner.

The souls did from their bodies fly,—
They fled to bliss or woe!
220   And every soul, it passed me by,
Like the whiz of my cross-bow!†

Part the Fourth.

The Wedding-Guest feareth that a spirit is talking to him;

"I fear thee, ancient Mariner!†
I fear thy skinny hand!
And thou art long, and lank, and brown,
225   As is the ribbed sea-sand.

"I fear thee and thy glittering eye,
And thy skinny hand, so brown—"

But the ancient Mariner assureth him of his bodily life, and proceedeth to relate his horrible penance.

Fear not, fear not, thou Wedding-Guest!
This body dropt not down.†

230   Alone, alone, all, all alone,
Alone on a wide wide sea!
And never a saint took pity on
My soul in agony.

The many men, so beautiful!
235 And they all dead did lie:
And a thousand thousand slimy things
Lived on—and so did I.

He despiseth the creatures of the calm.

I looked upon the rotting sea,
And drew my eyes away;
240 I looked upon the rotting deck,
And there the dead men lay.

And envieth that they should live, and so many lie dead.

I looked to Heaven, and tried to pray:
But or ever a prayer had gusht,
A wicked whisper came, and made
245 My heart as dry as dust.

I closed my lids, and kept them close,
And the balls like pulses beat;
For the sky and the sea, and the sea and the sky
Lay like a load on my weary eye,
250 And the dead were at my feet.

The cold sweat melted from their limbs,
Nor rot nor reek did they:
The look with which they looked on me
Had never passed away.†

But the curse liveth for him in the eye of the dead men.

255 An orphan's curse would drag to Hell
A spirit from on high;
But oh! more horrible than that
Is a curse in a dead man's eye!
Seven days, seven nights, I saw that curse,
260 And yet I could not die.

The moving Moon went up the sky,
And no where did abide:
Softly she was going up,
And a star or two beside.

In his loneliness and fixedness he yearneth towards the journeying Moon, and the stars that still sojourn, yet still move onward; and everywhere the blue sky belongs to them, and is their appointed rest and their native country and their own natural homes, which they enter unannounced, as lords that are certainly expected, and yet there is a silent joy at their arrival.

265   Her beams bemocked the sultry main,
Like April hoar-frost spread;
But where the ship's huge shadow lay,
The charmed water burnt alway
A still and awful red.

By the light of the Moon he beholdeth God's creatures of the great calm.

270   Beyond the shadow of the ship,
I watched the water-snakes:
They moved in tracks of shining white,
And when they reared, the elfish light
Fell off in hoary flakes.

275   Within the shadow of the ship
I watched their rich attire:
Blue, glossy green, and velvet black,
They coiled and swam; and every track
Was a flash of golden fire.

Their beauty and their happiness.

He blesseth them in his heart.

280   O happy living things! no tongue
Their beauty might declare:
A spring of love gushed from my heart,
And I blessed them unaware:
Sure my kind saint took pity on me,
285   And I blessed them unaware.†

The spell begins to break.

The selfsame moment I could pray;
And from my neck so free
The Albatross fell off, and sank
Like lead into the sea.

PART THE FIFTH.

290   Oh sleep! it is a gentle thing,
Beloved from pole to pole!
To Mary Queen† the praise be given!
She sent the gentle sleep from Heaven,
That slid into my soul.

By grace of the holy Mother, the ancient Mariner is refreshed with rain.

295   The silly buckets on the deck,
That had so long remained,
I dreamt that they were filled with dew;
And when I awoke, it rained.

My lips were wet, my throat was cold,
300 My garments all were dank;
Sure I had drunken in my dreams,
And still my body drank.

I moved, and could not feel my limbs:
I was so light—almost
305 I thought that I had died in sleep,
And was a blessed Ghost.

And soon I heard a roaring wind: *He heareth sounds and*
It did not come anear;   *seeth strange sights*
But with its sound it shook the sails,   *and commotions in the*
310 That were so thin and sere.   *sky and the element.*

The upper air burst into life!
And a hundred fire-flags sheen,
To and fro they were hurried about!
And to and fro, and in and out,
315 The wan stars danced between.

And the coming wind did roar more loud,
And the sails did sigh like sedge;
And the rain poured down from one black cloud;
The Moon was at its edge.

320 The thick black cloud was cleft and still
The Moon was at its side:
Like waters shot from some high crag,
The lightning fell with never a jag,
A river steep and wide.

325 The loud wind never reached the ship,   *The bodies of the ship's*
Yet now the ship moved on!   *crew are inspired, and*
Beneath the lightning and the Moon   *the ship moves on;*
The dead men gave a groan.

They groaned, they stirred, they all uprose,
330 Nor spake, nor moved their eyes;
It had been strange, even in a dream,
To have seen those dead men rise.†

The helmsman steered, the ship moved on;
Yet never a breeze up-blew;

335 The mariners all 'gan work the ropes,
Where they were wont to do:
They raised their limbs like lifeless tools—
We were a ghastly crew.

The body of my brother's son,
340 Stood by me, knee to knee:
The body and I pulled at one rope,
But he said nought to me.

But not by the souls of the men, nor by demons of earth or middle air, but by a blessed troop of angelic spirits, sent down by the invocation of the guardian saint.

"I fear thee, ancient Mariner!"
Be calm, thou Wedding-Guest!
345 'Twas not those souls that fled in pain,
Which to their corses came again,
But a troop of spirits blest:

For when it dawned—they dropped their arms,
And clustered round the mast;
350 Sweet sounds rose slowly through their mouths,
And from their bodies passed.

Around, around, flew each sweet sound,
Then darted to the Sun;
Slowly the sounds came back again,
355 Now mixed, now one by one.

Sometimes a-dropping from the sky
I heard the sky-lark sing;
Sometimes all little birds that are,
How they seemed to fill the sea and air
360 With their sweet jargoning!

And now 'twas like all instruments,
Now like a lonely flute;
And now it is an angel's song,
That makes the Heavens be mute.

365 It ceased; yet still the sails made on
      A pleasant noise till noon,
      A noise like of a hidden brook
      In the leafy month of June,
      That to the sleeping woods all night
370 Singeth a quiet tune.

      Till noon we quietly sailed on,
      Yet never a breeze did breathe:
      Slowly and smoothly went the ship,
      Moved onward from beneath.

375 Under the keel nine fathom deep,
      From the land of mist and snow,
      The spirit slid: and it was he
      That made the ship to go.[†]
      The sails at noon left off their tune,
380 And the ship stood still also.

The lonesome Spirit from the South Pole carries on the ship as far as the Line, in obedience to the angelic troop, but still requireth vengeance.

      The Sun, right up above the mast,
      Had fixed her to the ocean:
      But in a minute she 'gan stir,
      With a short uneasy motion—
385 Backwards and forwards half her length
      With a short uneasy motion.

      Then like a pawing horse let go,
      She made a sudden bound:
      It flung the blood into my head,
390 And I fell down in a swound.

      How long in that same fit I lay,
      I have not to declare;
      But ere my living life returned,
      I heard and in my soul discerned
395 Two voices in the air.

      "Is it he?" quoth one, "Is this the man?
      By him who died on cross,[†]
      With his cruel bow he laid full low,
      The harmless Albatross.

The Polar Spirit's fellow-demons, the invisible inhabitants of the element, take part in his wrong; and two of them relate, one to the other, that penance long and heavy for the ancient Mariner hath been accorded to the Polar Spirit, who returneth southward.

400 "The spirit who bideth by himself
  In the land of mist and snow,
  He loved the bird that loved the man
  Who shot him with his bow."

  The other was a softer voice,
405 As soft as honey-dew:
  Quoth he, "The man hath penance done,
  And penance more will do."

PART THE SIXTH.

FIRST VOICE.

  But tell me, tell me! speak again,
  Thy soft response renewing—
410 What makes that ship drive on so fast?
  What is the Ocean doing?

SECOND VOICE.

  Still as a slave before his lord,
  The Ocean hath no blast;
  His great bright eye most silently
415 Up to the Moon is cast—

  If he may know which way to go;
  For she guides him smooth or grim
  See, brother, see! how graciously
  She looketh down on him.

FIRST VOICE.

The Mariner hath 420 But why drives on that ship so fast,
been cast into a   Without or wave or wind?
trance; for the angelic
power causeth the ves-
sel to drive northward   SECOND VOICE.
faster than human life
could endure.   The air is cut away before,
  And closes from behind.

Fly, brother, fly! more high, more high
425 Or we shall be belated:
For slow and slow that ship will go,
When the Mariner's trance is abated.

I woke, and we were sailing on
As in a gentle weather:
430 'Twas night, calm night, the Moon was high;
The dead men stood together.

*The supernatural
motion is retarded; the
Mariner awakes, and
his penance begins
anew.*

All stood together on the deck,
For a charnel-dungeon fitter:†
All fixed on me their stony eyes,
435 That in the Moon did glitter.

The pang, the curse, with which they died,
Had never passed away:
I could not draw my eyes from theirs,
Nor turn them up to pray.

440 And now this spell was snapt: once more
I viewed the ocean green.
And looked far forth, yet little saw
Of what had else been seen—

*The curse is finally
expiated.*

Like one that on a lonesome road
445 Doth walk in fear and dread,
And having once turned round walks on,
And turns no more his head;
Because he knows, a frightful fiend
Doth close behind him tread.

450 But soon there breathed a wind on me,
Nor sound nor motion made:
Its path was not upon the sea,
In ripple or in shade.

It raised my hair, it fanned my cheek
455 Like a meadow-gale of spring—
It mingled strangely with my fears,
Yet it felt like a welcoming.

Swiftly, swiftly flew the ship,
Yet she sailed softly too:
460 Sweetly, sweetly blew the breeze—
On me alone it blew.

And the ancient Mariner beholdeth his native country.

Oh! dream of joy! is this indeed
The light-house top I see?
Is this the hill? is this the kirk?
465 Is this mine own countree!

We drifted o'er the harbour-bar,
And I with sobs did pray—
O let me be awake, my God!
Or let me sleep alway.

470 The harbour-bay was clear as glass,
So smoothly it was strewn!
And on the bay the moonlight lay,
And the shadow of the Moon.

The rock shone bright, the kirk no less,
475 That stands above the rock:
The moonlight steeped in silentness
The steady weathercock.

The angelic spirits leave the dead bodies,

And the bay was white with silent light,
Till rising from the same,
480 Full many shapes, that shadows were,
In crimson colours came.

And appear in their own forms of light.

A little distance from the prow
Those crimson shadows were:
I turned my eyes upon the deck—
485 Oh, Christ! what saw I there!

Each corse lay flat, lifeless and flat,
And, by the holy rood!†
A man all light, a seraph-man,†
On every corse there stood.

490 This seraph band, each waved his hand:
It was a heavenly sight!
They stood as signals to the land,
Each one a lovely light:

This seraph-band, each waved his hand,
495 No voice did they impart—
No voice; but oh! the silence sank
Like music on my heart.

But soon I heard the dash of oars;
I heard the Pilot's cheer;
500 My head was turned perforce away,
And I saw a boat appear.

The Pilot, and the Pilot's boy,
I heard them coming fast:
Dear Lord in Heaven! it was a joy
505 The dead men could not blast.

I saw a third—I heard his voice:
It is the Hermit good!†
He singeth loud his godly hymns
That he makes in the wood.
510 He'll shrieve my soul, he'll wash away
The Albatross's blood.

PART THE SEVENTH.

This Hermit good lives in that wood   *The Hermit of the*
Which slopes down to the sea.   *Wood.*
How loudly his sweet voice he rears!
515 He loves to talk with marineres
That come from a far countree.

He kneels at morn and noon and eve—
He hath a cushion plump:
It is the moss that wholly hides
520 The rotted old oak-stump.

The skiff-boat neared: I heard them talk,
"Why this is strange, I trow!
Where are those lights so many and fair,
That signal made but now?"

Approacheth the ship
with wonder.

525 "Strange, by my faith!" the Hermit said[†]—
"And they answered not our cheer!
The planks looked warped! and see those sails,
How thin they are and sere!
I never saw aught like to them,
530 Unless perchance it were

"Brown skeletons of leaves that lag
My forest-brook along;
When the ivy-tod is heavy with snow,
And the owlet whoops to the wolf below,
535 That eats the she-wolf's young."

"Dear Lord! it hath a fiendish look—
(The Pilot made reply)
I am a-feared"—"Push on, push on!"
Said the Hermit cheerily.

540 The boat came closer to the ship,
But I nor spake nor stirred;
The boat came close beneath the ship,
And straight a sound was heard.

The ship suddenly
sinketh.

Under the water it rumbled on,
545 Still louder and more dread:
It reached the ship, it split the bay;
The ship went down like lead.

The ancient Mariner
is saved in the Pilot's
boat.

Stunned by that loud and dreadful sound,
Which sky and ocean smote,
550 Like one that hath been seven days drowned
My body lay afloat;
But swift as dreams, myself I found
Within the Pilot's boat.

Upon the whirl, where sank the ship,
555   The boat spun round and round;
And all was still, save that the hill
Was telling of the sound.

I moved my lips—the Pilot shrieked
And fell down in a fit;
560   The holy Hermit raised his eyes,
And prayed where he did sit.

I took the oars: the Pilot's boy,
Who now doth crazy go,
Laughed loud and long, and all the while
565   His eyes went to and fro.
"Ha! ha!" quoth he, "full plain I see,
The Devil knows how to row."

And now, all in my own countree,
I stood on the firm land!
570   The Hermit stepped forth from the boat,
And scarcely he could stand.

"O shrieve me, shrieve me, holy man!"   *The ancient Mariner*
The Hermit crossed his brow.   *earnestly entreateth*
"Say quick," quoth he, "I bid thee say—   *the Hermit to shrieve*
                                                him; and the penance
575   What manner of man art thou?"   *of life falls on him.*

Forthwith this frame of mine was wrenched
With a woeful agony,
Which forced me to begin my tale;
And then it left me free.

580   Since then, at an uncertain hour,   *And ever and anon*
That agony returns;   *throughout his future*
                                                life an agony con-
And till my ghastly tale is told,   *straineth him to travel*
This heart within me burns.†   *from land to land;*

I pass, like night, from land to land;
585   I have strange power of speech;
That moment that his face I see,
I know the man that must hear me:
To him my tale I teach.

What loud uproar bursts from that door!
590   The wedding-guests are there:
But in the garden-bower the bride
And bride-maids singing are:
And hark the little vesper bell,
Which biddeth me to prayer!

595   O Wedding-Guest! this soul hath been
Alone on a wide wide sea:
So lonely 'twas, that God himself
Scarce seemed there to be.

O sweeter than the marriage-feast,
600   'Tis sweeter far to me,
To walk together to the kirk
With a goodly company!—

To walk together to the kirk,
And all together pray,
605   While each to his great Father bends,
Old men, and babes, and loving friends,
And youths and maidens gay!

And to teach, by his own example, love and reverence to all things that God made and loveth.

Farewell, farewell! but this I tell
To thee, thou Wedding-Guest!
610   He prayeth well, who loveth well
Both man and bird and beast.

He prayeth best, who loveth best
All things both great and small;
For the dear God who loveth us
615   He made and loveth all.

The Mariner, whose eye is bright,
Whose beard with age is hoar,
Is gone: and now the Wedding-Guest
Turned from the bridegroom's door.

620   He went like one that hath been stunned,
And is of sense forlorn:
A sadder and a wiser man,
He rose the morrow morn.†

Kubla Khan

Or, A Vision in a Dream. A Fragment.[†]

In Xanadu[†] did Kubla Khan[†]
A stately pleasure-dome decree:
Where Alph,[†] the sacred river, ran
Through caverns measureless to man
     Down to a sunless sea.
So twice five miles of fertile ground
With walls and towers were girdled round:
And there were gardens bright with sinuous rills,
Where blossomed many an incense-bearing tree;
And here were forests ancient as the hills,
Enfolding sunny spots of greenery.

     But oh! that deep romantic chasm which slanted
     Down the green hill athwart a cedarn cover!
     A savage place! as holy and enchanted
     As e'er beneath a waning moon was haunted
     By woman wailing for her demon-lover!
     And from this chasm, with ceaseless turmoil seething,
     As if this earth in fast thick pants were breathing,
     A mighty fountain momently was forced:
     Amid whose swift half-intermitted burst
     Huge fragments vaulted like rebounding hail,
     Or chaffy grain beneath the thresher's flail:[†]
     And 'mid these dancing rocks at once and ever
     It flung up momently the sacred river.

Five miles meandering with a mazy motion
Through wood and dale the sacred river ran,
Then reached the caverns measureless to man,
And sank in tumult to a lifeless ocean:
And 'mid this tumult Kubla heard from far
Ancestral voices prophesying war!

The shadow of the dome of pleasure
Floated midway on the waves;
Where was heard the mingled measure
From the fountain and the caves.
It was a miracle of rare device,
A sunny pleasure-dome with caves of ice!
A damsel with a dulcimer
In a vision once I saw:
It was an Abyssinian† maid,
And on her dulcimer she played,
Singing of Mount Abora.†
Could I revive within me
Her symphony and song,
To such a deep delight 'twould win me,
That with music loud and long,
I would build that dome in air,
That sunny dome! those caves of ice!
And all who heard should see them there,
And all should cry, Beware! Beware!
His flashing eyes, his floating hair!
Weave a circle round him thrice,
And close your eyes with holy dread,
For he on honey-dew hath fed,
And drunk the milk of Paradise.†

WILLIAM BLAKE

"If the doors of perception were cleansed, every thing would appear to man as it is, infinite"

—WILLIAM BLAKE
The Marriage of Heaven and Hell

WILLIAM BLAKE WAS BORN on November 28, 1757, to a middle-class family in London. His father was a hosier, and his mother took primary responsibility for Blake's education. The Blakes were Dissenters and may have belonged to either the Moravian sect or the Muggletonians. Both were Protestant sects that focused more on an individual's right to read and interpret the scripture than on the need of a priest to instruct the faithful. The Bible was a strong early influence on Blake and would continue to be so throughout his life.

Like the founders of the Muggletonian sect, Blake claimed to see visions. His first was when he was eight or ten years old, and he reported seeing a tree filled with angels "bespangling every bough like stars." This visionary and mystical aspect of religion would become a significant element in Blake's art and poetry.

As a young man, Blake was apprenticed to learn the engraver's trade, and he would forever combine his engraving, printing, and poetic arts into a single form, claiming that the text was incomplete without the illustration and vice versa.

In 1782, after a refused proposal of marriage, Blake met and married Catherine Boucher, who would become his most powerful ally and assistant for the rest of his life.

As a writer during this period of revolution (the American Revolution began in 1776 and the French Revolution in 1789), Blake became friends with William Wordsworth and William and Mary (Wollstonecraft) Godwin (parents of Mary Shelley). Blake abhorred slavery and believed in racial and sexual equality. He had great hopes for the revolutions in the United States and France and was extremely disillusioned by the Reign of Terror and the rise of Napoleon.

Following her husband's death on August 12, 1827, Catherine claimed that Blake would come and sit with her for two or three hours every day. She continued selling his paintings and illuminated poems, but would transact no business without first consulting her late husband. On the day of her own death, in October 1831, she was calm and cheerful, and called out to him "as if he were only in the next room, to say she was coming to him, and it would not be long now."

Blake was an important proponent of imagination. He believed that the creative force would allow humanity to overcome the limitations of its five senses. In addition to being regarded an early Romantic poet, Blake is celebrated as a forerunner of the "expanded consciousness" movement of the twentieth century. Aldous Huxley took the name of one of his most famous works, *The Doors of Perception,* from one of Blake's most famous works, and the rock group *The Doors* took their name from Huxley's work.

The Lamb

From *Songs of Innocence*[†]

Little lamb, who made thee?
Does thou know who made thee,
Gave thee life, & bid thee feed
By the stream & o'er the mead;
Gave thee clothing of delight,
Softest clothing, woolly, bright;
Gave thee such a tender voice,
Making all the vales rejoice?
Little lamb, who made thee?
Does thou know who made thee?

Little lamb, I'll tell thee;
Little lamb, I'll tell thee:
He is called by thy name,[†]
For He calls Himself a Lamb.
He is meek, & He is mild,
He became a little child.[†]
I a child, & thou a lamb,[†]
We are called by His name.
Little lamb, God bless thee!
Little lamb, God bless thee!

The Tyger

From *Songs of Experience*[†]

Tyger! Tyger! burning bright
In the forests of the night,
What immortal hand or eye
Could frame thy fearful symmetry?

In what distant deeps or skies
Burnt the fire of thine eyes?
On what wings dare he aspire?
What the hand dare seize the fire?

And what shoulder & what art
Could twist the sinews of thy heart?
And, when thy heart began to beat,
What dread hand & what dread feet?

What the hammer? what the chain?
In what furnace was thy brain?[†]
What the anvil? what dread grasp
Dare its deadly terrors clasp?

When the stars threw down their spears,
And watered heaven with their tears,
Did He smile His work to see?
Did He who made the lamb make thee?[†]

Tyger! Tyger! burning bright
In the forests of the night,
What immortal hand or eye
Dare frame thy fearful symmetry?

The Chimney Sweeper

From *Songs of Innocence*

When my mother died I was very young,
And my father sold me while yet my tongue
Could scarcely cry " 'weep! 'weep! 'weep! 'weep!'†
So your chimneys I sweep, and in soot I sleep.

There's little Tom Dacre, who cried when his head,
That curled like a lamb's back, was shaved;† so I said,'
Hush, Tom! never mind it, for, when your head's bare,
You know that the soot cannot spoil your white hair.'

And so he was quiet, & that very night,
As Tom was a-sleeping, he had such a sight!—
That thousands of sweepers, Dick, Joe, Ned, & Jack,
Were all of them locked up in coffins of black.

And by came an angel, who had a bright key,
And he opened the coffins, & set them all free;
Then down a green plain, leaping, laughing, they run
And wash in a river, and shine in the sun.

Then naked & white, all their bags† left behind,
They rise upon clouds, and sport in the wind:
And the angel told Tom, if he'd be a good boy,
He'd have God for his father, & never want joy.

And so Tom awoke, and we rose in the dark,
And got with our bags & our brushes to work.
Though the morning was cold, Tom was happy & warm:
So, if all do their duty, they need not fear harm.†

The Chimney Sweeper

From *Songs of Experience*

A little black thing among the snow,
Crying " 'weep! 'weep," in notes of woe!
"Where are thy father & mother? Say?"
"They are both gone up to the church to pray.

"Because I was happy upon the heath,
And smiled among the winter's snow,
They clothed me in the clothes of death,
And taught me to sing the notes of woe.

"And because I am happy & dance & sing,
They think they have done me no injury,
And are gone to praise God & his Priest & King,
Who made up a heaven of our misery."

A Poison Tree

From *Songs of Experience*

I was angry with my friend:
I told my wrath, my wrath did end.
I was angry with my foe:
I told it not, my wrath did grow.

And I watered it in fears
Night & morning with my tears,
And I sunnéd it with smiles
And with soft deceitful wiles.

And it grew both day and night,
Till it bore an apple bright,[†]
And my foe beheld it shine,
And he knew that it was mine,

And into my garden stole
When the night had veiled the pole;[†]
In the morning, glad, I see
My foe outstretched beneath the tree.

WILLIAM WORDSWORTH

We have within ourselves
Enough to fill the present day with joy,
And overspread the future years with hope.

—WILLIAM WORDSWORTH
The Recluse

WILLIAM WORDSWORTH WAS BORN on April 7, 1770, in the Lake District of England. After the death of their mother in 1778 and their father in 1783, Wordsworth and his siblings were brought up under the guardianship of their uncles. Wordsworth would later describe frequent bouts of depression and persistent grief for the deaths of his parents and a subsequent separation from his brothers and sisters. As adults, he and his sister Dorothy would become inseparable friends.

Wordsworth toured France in 1791 and fell in love with Annette Vallon, with whom he had a daughter, Caroline. Wordsworth would most likely have married Annette, but the Revolution in France made it impossible for him to stay there, and growing conflict between France and England forced him to take his family home to England. He did, however, support Annette and Caroline for the rest of their lives.

Like William Blake, Wordsworth had been an early supporter of the French Revolution, but was disheartened by the horrible excesses of the Reign of Terror.

He met Samuel Taylor Coleridge in 1793, and the two poets became close friends. Together, Wordsworth and Coleridge wrote *Lyrical Ballads*, a collection of poems that many credit as beginning the English Romantic movement. In *Lyrical Ballads*, Wordsworth and Coleridge attempted to depart from the highly eloquent and stylistic works of the Enlightenment and develop a new form, based on the "real language of men." The collection includes Wordsworth's "Tintern Abbey," and Coleridge's "Rime of the Ancient Mariner."

By 1804, Wordsworth's friendship with Coleridge had begun to deteriorate, largely due to Wordsworth's concern about Coleridge's opium addiction and Coleridge's disillusionment that Wordsworth was losing the liberal idealism that had once driven his work. The poets' friendship, especially their collaboration on *Lyrical Ballads*, is explored in the 2000 film, *Pandaemonium*.

Wordsworth expected to be named England's Poet Laureate in 1813, but lost the title to his friend Robert Southey (who is best known today as the author of "Goldilocks and the Three Bears"). When Southey died in 1843, Wordsworth was finally appointed to the post.

After his death on April 23, 1850, Wordsworth's widow published the long autobiographical "poem to Coleridge" under the title *The Prelude*. It did not meet with either critical or commercial success on its original publication, but it is now generally regarded as Wordsworth's masterpiece.

Lines
Composed a Few Miles above Tintern Abbey, on Revisiting the Banks of the Wye[†] during a Tour, July 13, 1798

From *Lyrical Ballads*

Five years have passed; five summers, with the length
Of five long winters! and again I hear
These waters, rolling from their mountain-springs
With a sweet inland murmur.—Once again
Do I behold these steep and lofty cliffs,
Which on a wild secluded scene impress
Thoughts of more deep seclusion; and connect
The landscape with the quiet of the sky.
The day is come when I again repose
Here, under this dark sycamore, and view
These plots of cottage-ground, these orchard-tufts,
Which, at this season, with their unripe fruits,
Among the woods and copses lose themselves,
Nor, with their green and simple hue, disturb
The wild green landscape.[†] Once again I see
These hedge-rows, hardly hedge-rows, little lines
Of sportive wood run wild; these pastoral farms
Green to the very door; and wreaths of smoke
Sent up, in silence, from among the trees,
With some uncertain notice, as might seem,
Of vagrant dwellers in the houseless woods,
Or of some hermit's cave,[†] where by his fire
The hermit sits alone.

　　　　　Though absent long,
These forms of beauty have not been to me,
As is a landscape to a blind man's eye:[†]

But oft, in lonely rooms, and 'mid the din
Of towns and cities, I have owed to them,
In hours of weariness, sensations sweet,
Felt in the blood,[†] and felt along the heart,
And passing even into my purer mind
With tranquil restoration:—feelings too
Of unremembered pleasure; such, perhaps,
As may have had no trivial influence[†]
On that best portion of a good man's life;
His little, nameless, unremembered acts
Of kindness and of love.[†] Nor less, I trust,
To them I may have owed another gift,
Of aspect more sublime; that blessed mood,
In which the burthen of the mystery,
In which the heavy and the weary weight
Of all this unintelligible world
Is lightened[†]:— that serene and blessed mood,
In which the affections gently lead us on,
Until, the breath of this corporeal frame,
And even the motion of our human blood
Almost suspended, we are laid asleep
In body, and become a living soul:[†]
While with an eye made quiet by the power
Of harmony, and the deep power of joy,
We see into the life of things.

      If this
Be but a vain belief, yet, oh! how oft–
In darkness, and amid the many shapes
Of joyless daylight; when the fretful stir
Unprofitable, and the fever of the world,
Have hung upon the beatings of my heart–
How oft, in spirit, have I turned to thee
O sylvan Wye! Thou wanderer through the woods,
How often has my spirit turned to thee!

And now, with gleams of half-extinguished thought,
With many recognitions dim and faint,
And somewhat of a sad perplexity,
The picture of the mind revives again:
While here I stand, not only with the sense
Of present pleasure, but with pleasing thoughts

That in this moment there is life and food
For future years.† And so I dare to hope
Though changed, no doubt, from what I was, when first
I came among these hills; when like a roe
I bounded o'er the mountains, by the sides
Of the deep rivers, and the lonely streams,
Wherever nature led; more like a man
Flying from something that he dreads, than one
Who sought the thing he loved. For nature then
(The coarser pleasures of my boyish days,
And their glad animal movements all gone by,)
To me was all in all.— I cannot paint
What then I was. The sounding cataract
Haunted me like a passion: the tall rock,
The mountain, and the deep and gloomy wood,
Their colours and their forms, were then to me
An appetite: a feeling and a love,
That had no need of a remoter charm,
By thought supplied, or any interest
Unborrowed from the eye.—That time is past,
And all its aching joys are now no more,
And all its dizzy raptures. Not for this
Faint I, nor mourn nor murmur:† other gifts
Have followed, for such loss, I would believe,
Abundant recompense.† For I have learned
To look on nature, not as in the hour
Of thoughtless youth, but hearing oftentimes
The still, sad music of humanity,
Not harsh nor grating, though of ample power
To chasten and subdue. And I have felt
A presence that disturbs me with the joy
Of elevated thoughts; a sense sublime
Of something far more deeply interfused,
Whose dwelling is the light of setting suns,
And the round ocean, and the living air,
And the blue sky, and in the mind of man,
A motion and a spirit, that impels
All thinking things, all objects of all thought,
And rolls through all things. Therefore am I still
A lover of the meadows and the woods,
And mountains; and of all that we behold

From this green earth; of all the mighty world
Of eye and ear, both what they half-create,
And what perceive; well pleased to recognize
In nature and the language of the sense,
The anchor of my purest thoughts, the nurse,
The guide, the guardian of my heart, and soul
Of all my moral being.

        Nor, perchance,
If I were not thus taught, should I the more
Suffer my genial spirits to decay:
For thou[†] art with me, here, upon the banks
Of this fair river; thou, my dearest Friend,
My dear, dear Friend, and in thy voice I catch
The language of my former heart, and read
My former pleasures in the shooting lights
Of thy wild eyes. Oh! yet a little while
May I behold in thee what I was once,
My dear, dear Sister! And this prayer I make,
Knowing that Nature never did betray
The heart that loved her; 'tis her privilege,
Through all the years of this our life, to lead
From joy to joy: for she can so inform
The mind that is within us, so impress
With quietness and beauty, and so feed
With lofty thoughts, that neither evil tongues,
Rash judgments, nor the sneers of selfish men,
Nor greetings where no kindness is, nor all
The dreary intercourse of daily life,
Shall e'er prevail against us, or disturb
Our cheerful faith that all which we behold
Is full of blessings. Therefore let the moon
Shine on thee in thy solitary walk;
And let the misty mountain winds be free
To blow against thee: and in after years,
When these wild ecstasies shall be matured
Into a sober pleasure, when thy mind
Shall be a mansion for all lovely forms,
Thy memory be as a dwelling-place
For all sweet sounds and harmonies;[†] Oh! then,
If solitude, or fear, or pain, or grief,

Should be thy portion, with what healing thoughts
Of tender joy wilt thou remember me,
And these my exhortations! Nor, perchance–
If I should be, where I no more can hear
Thy voice, nor catch from thy wild eyes these gleams
Of past existence–wilt thou then forget
That on the banks of this delightful stream
We stood together; and that I, so long
A worshipper of Nature, hither came,
Unwearied in that service: rather say
With warmer love–oh! with far deeper zeal
Of holier love. Nor wilt thou then forget,
That after many wanderings, many years
Of absence, these steep woods and lofty cliffs,
And this green pastoral landscape, were to me
More dear, both for themselves, and for thy sake.

My Heart Leaps Up

My heart leaps up when I behold
    A rainbow in the sky:
So was it when my life began,
So is it now I am a man,
So be it when I shall grow old
    Or let me die!
The child is father of the man:
And I could wish my days to be
Bound each to each by natural piety†

Ode:
Intimations of Immortality from Recollections of Early Childhood

I

There was a time when meadow, grove, and stream,
The earth, and every common sight,
  To me did seem
  Apparelled in celestial light,
The glory and the freshness of a dream.
It is not now as it hath been of yore;—
  Turn wheresoe'er I may,
  By night or day,
The things which I have seen I now can see no more.

II

  The Rainbow† comes and goes,
  And lovely is the Rose,
  The Moon doth with delight
Look round her when the heavens are bare,
  Waters on a starry night
  Are beautiful and fair;
 The sunshine is a glorious birth;
 But yet I know, where'er I go,
That there hath past away a glory from the earth.

III

Now, while the birds thus sing a joyous song,
  And while the young lambs bound
  As to the tabor's sound,
To me alone there came a thought of grief:
A timely utterance gave that thought relief,
  And I again am strong:
The cataracts blow their trumpets from the steep;
No more shall grief of mine the season wrong;

I hear the Echoes through the mountains throng,
The Winds come to me from the fields of sleep,
 And all the earth is gay;
  Land and sea
 Give themselves up to jollity,
  And with the heart of May
 Doth every Beast keep holiday;—
  Thou Child of Joy,
Shout round me, let me hear thy shouts, thou happy
 Shepherd-boy!†

IV

Ye blesséd Creatures, I have heard the call
 Ye to each other make; I see
The heavens laugh with you in your jubilee;
 My heart is at your festival,
 My head hath its coronal,
The fulness of your bliss, I feel—I feel it all.
  Oh evil day! if I were sullen
  While Earth herself is adorning,
  This sweet May-morning,
 And the Children are culling
  On every side,
 In a thousand valleys far and wide,
  Fresh flowers; while the sun shines warm,
And the Babe leaps up on his Mother's arm:—
 I hear, I hear, with joy I hear!
 —But there's a Tree, of many, one,
A single Field which I have looked upon,
Both of them speak of something that is gone:†
 The Pansy at my feet
 Doth the same tale repeat:
Whither is fled the visionary gleam?†
Where is it now, the glory and the dream?

V

Our birth is but a sleep and a forgetting:†
The Soul that rises with us, our life's Star,
 Hath had elsewhere its setting,
  And cometh from afar:
 Not in entire forgetfulness,

And not in utter nakedness,
But trailing clouds of glory[†] do we come
   From God, who is our home:
Heaven lies about us in our infancy!
Shades[†] of the prison-house begin to close
   Upon the growing Boy,
But He beholds the light,[†] and whence it flows,
   He sees it in his joy;
The Youth, who daily farther from the east
   Must travel, still is Nature's Priest,[†]
   And by the vision splendid[†]
   Is on his way attended;
At length the Man perceives it die away,
And fade into the light of common day.

VI

Earth fills her lap with pleasures of her own;
Yearnings she hath in her own natural kind,
And, even with something of a Mother's mind,[†]
   And no unworthy aim,
   The homely Nurse doth all she can
To make her Foster-child,[†] her Inmate[†] Man,
   Forget the glories he hath known,
And that imperial palace whence he came.

VII

Behold the Child among his new-born blisses,
A six years' Darling of a pigmy size!
See, where 'mid work of his own hand he lies,
Fretted by sallies of his mother's kisses,
With light upon him from his father's eyes!
See, at his feet, some little plan or chart,
Some fragment from his dream of human life,
Shaped by himself with newly-learned art;
   A wedding or a festival,
   A mourning or a funeral;
   And this hath now his heart,
   And unto this he frames his song:
   Then will he fit his tongue
To dialogues of business, love, or strife;
   But it will not be long

Ere this be thrown aside,
And with new joy and pride
The little Actor cons another part;
Filling from time to time his "humorous stage"
With all the Persons, down to palsied Age,
That Life brings with her in her equipage;
As if his whole vocation
Were endless imitation.

VIII

Thou, whose exterior semblance doth belie
Thy Soul's immensity;[†]
Thou best Philosopher, who yet dost keep
Thy heritage, thou Eye among the blind,[†]
That, deaf and silent, read'st the eternal deep,
Haunted for ever by the eternal mind,—
Mighty Prophet! Seer blest!
On whom those truths do rest,
Which we are toiling all our lives to find,
In darkness lost, the darkness of the grave;
Thou, over whom thy Immortality
Broods like the Day, a Master o'er a Slave,
A Presence which is not to be put by;
Thou little Child, yet glorious in the might
Of heaven-born freedom on thy being's height,
Why with such earnest pains dost thou provoke
The years to bring the inevitable yoke,
Thus blindly with thy blessedness at strife?
Full soon thy Soul shall have her earthly freight,
And custom lie upon thee with a weight
Heavy as frost, and deep almost as life!

IX

O joy! that in our embers
Is something that doth live,
That nature yet remembers
What was so fugitive!
The thought of our past years in me doth breed
Perpetual benediction:[†] not indeed
For that which is most worthy to be blest—
Delight and liberty, the simple creed
Of Childhood, whether busy or at rest,

With new-fledged hope still fluttering in his breast:—
    Not for these I raise
    The song of thanks and praise;
    But for those obstinate questionings
    Of sense and outward things,[†]
    Fallings from us, vanishings;
    Blank misgivings of a Creature
Moving about in worlds not realised,
High instincts before which our mortal Nature
Did tremble like a guilty Thing surprised:
    But for those first affections,
    Those shadowy recollections,
    Which, be they what they may,
Are yet the fountain light of all our day,
Are yet a master light of all our seeing;
    Uphold us, cherish, and have power to make
Our noisy years seem moments in the being
Of the eternal Silence: truths that wake,
      To perish never;
Which neither listlessness, nor mad endeavour,
      Nor Man nor Boy,
Nor all that is at enmity with joy,
Can utterly abolish or destroy!
 Hence in a season of calm weather
    Though inland far we be,
Our Souls have sight of that immortal sea[†]
    Which brought us hither,
Can in a moment travel thither,
And see the Children sport upon the shore,
And hear the mighty waters rolling evermore.

          X
Then sing, ye Birds, sing, sing a joyous song!
    And let the young Lambs bound
    As to the tabor's sound!
We in thought will join your throng,
    Ye that pipe and ye that play,
    Ye that through your hearts to-day
    Feel the gladness of the May!
What though the radiance which was once so bright
Be now for ever taken from my sight,
  Though nothing can bring back the hour

Of splendour in the grass, of glory in the flower;
    We will grieve not, rather find
    Strength in what remains behind;
    In the primal sympathy†
    Which having been must ever be;
    In the soothing thoughts that spring
    Out of human suffering;
    In the faith that looks through death,
In years that bring the philosophic mind.

XI

And O, ye Fountains, Meadows, Hills, and Groves,
Forebode not any severing of our loves!
Yet in my heart of hearts I feel your might;
I only have relinquished one delight
To live beneath your more habitual sway.
I love the Brooks which down their channels fret,
Even more than when I tripped lightly as they;
The innocent brightness of a new-born Day
        Is lovely yet;
The Clouds that gather round the setting sun
Do take a sober colouring from an eye
That hath kept watch o'er man's mortality;
Another race hath been, and other palms are won.
Thanks to the human heart by which we live,
Thanks to its tenderness, its joys, and fears,
To me the meanest flower that blows can give
Thoughts that do often lie too deep for tears.

The Lucy Poems †

STRANGE FITS OF PASSION HAVE I KNOWN

Strange fits of passion† have I known,
And I will dare to tell,
But in the lover's ear alone,
What once to me befel.

When she I loved looked every day
Fresh as a rose in June,
I to her cottage bent my way,
Beneath an evening moon.

Upon the moon I fixed my eye,
All over the wide lea;
With quickening pace my horse drew nigh
Those paths so dear to me.

And now we reached the orchard-plot,
And, as we climbed the hill,
The sinking moon to Lucy's cot
Came near, and nearer still.

In one of those sweet dreams I slept,
Kind Nature's gentlest boon!
And, all the while, my eyes I kept
On the descending moon.

My horse moved on; hoof after hoof
He raised, and never stopped:
When down behind the cottage roof
At once, the bright moon dropped.†

What fond and wayward thoughts will slide
Into a Lover's head!
"O mercy!" to myself I cried,
"If Lucy should be dead!"

SHE DWELT AMONG THE UNTRODDEN WAYS

She dwelt among the untrodden ways
   Beside the springs of Dove,[†]
A Maid whom there were none to praise
   And very few to love.

A violet by a mossy stone
   Half-hidden from the Eye!
—Fair, as a star when only one
   Is shining in the sky.

She lived unknown, and few could know
   When Lucy ceased to be;
But she is in her Grave, and, oh,
   The difference to me!

I TRAVELLED AMONG UNKNOWN MEN

I travelled among unknown men,
  In lands beyond the sea;
Nor, England! did I know till then
  What love I bore to thee.[†]

'Tis past, that melancholy dream!
  Nor will I quit thy shore
A second time; for still I seem
  To love thee more and more.

Among thy mountains did I feel
  The joy of my desire;
And she I cherished turned her wheel
  Beside an English fire.

Thy mornings showed, thy nights concealed
  The bowers where Lucy played;
And thine too is the last green field[†]
  That Lucy's eyes surveyed.

THREE YEARS SHE GREW IN SUN AND SHOWER

Three years she grew in sun and shower,
Then Nature said, "A lovelier flower
On earth was never sown;
This Child I to myself will take,
She shall be mine, and I will make
A Lady of my own.

"Myself will to my darling be
Both law and impulse, and with me
The Girl, in rock and plain,
In earth and heaven, in glade and bower,
Shall feel an overseeing power
To kindle or restrain.

"She shall be sportive as the fawn
That wild with glee across the lawn
Or up the mountain springs;
And hers shall be the breathing balm,
And hers the silence and the calm
Of mute insensate things.

"The floating clouds their state shall lend
To her; for her the willow bend,
Nor shall she fail to see
Even in the motions of the Storm
Grace that shall mould the Maiden's form
By silent sympathy.

"The stars of midnight shall be dear
To her; and she shall lean her ear
In many a secret place
Where rivulets dance their wayward round,
And beauty born of murmuring sound
Shall pass into her face.

"And vital feelings of delight
Shall rear her form to stately height,
Her virgin bosom swell,
Such thoughts to Lucy I will give
While she and I together live
Here in this happy dell."

Thus Nature spake—the work was done—
How soon my Lucy's race was run!
She died and left to me
This heath, this calm and quiet scene,
The memory of what has been,
And never more will be.†

A SLUMBER DID MY SPIRIT SEAL

A slumber did my spirit seal;
   I had no human fears:
She seemed a thing that could not feel
   The touch of earthly years.

No motion has she now, no force;
   She neither hears nor sees;
Rolled round in earth's diurnal course
   With rocks, and stones, and trees!

GEORGE GORDON, LORD BYRON

If I should meet thee
After long years,
How should I greet thee?
With silence and tears.

— GEORGE GORDON, LORD BYRON
"When We Two Parted"

G EORGE GORDON, LORD BYRON was born in London on January 22, 1788. His father was a ne'er-do-well soldier of fortune who fought continually with his wife, Lady Catherine Gordon and left before his son was born. Eventually, he was killed in the French Revolution.

Byron suffered from a malformation of the right foot, causing a slight limp. As an adult, he wore special boots to hide the deformity of his foot and the smallness of his calf muscle.

Despite Lady Catherine's title and lineage, Byron and his mother lived in near poverty—her father had committed suicide in 1779, leaving enormous debts, and Byron's father had squandered what little was left of Lady Catherine's fortune—until 1798 when George Gordon became the sixth Baron Byron (Lord Byron) upon the death of his mother's uncle.

While rapidly becoming famous as a poet, Byron was also becoming infamous for his affairs. Eventually, his dalliances would bring so much criticism from his colleagues in the House of Lords and the general populace that he would admit to being afraid to ride in his carriage or attend the theater for fear of being accosted. In 1814, his half-sister, with whom he was very close, had a daughter who was commonly assumed to have been Byron's. When his marriage to Anne Isabella ("Annabella") Milbanke ended in 1816 amid rumors of domestic violence and adultery, Byron left England forever.

During the summer of 1816, the Byron-Shelley party, which included Byron's personal physician John Polidori, conceived the ghost-story contest that would result in Mary Shelley's writing *Frankenstein* and Polidori's writing *The Vampire*.

Byron also made significant progress on two of his most famous works, *Childe Harold's Pilgrimage* and *Manfred*, and he began the work he would not live to finish, *Don Juan*.

In 1823, he offered support to Greek insurgents, who were fighting for their independence from the Ottoman Empire. He spent a considerable sum of money from his own fortune refitting the Greek fleet and paying soldiers' salaries. He hoped to lead a unit into combat himself; but, before he was able to experience any action, he fell seriously ill.

Byron died in Greece on April 19, 1824.

On the Castle of Chillon[†]

Eternal Spirit of the chainless Mind!
Brightest in dungeons, Liberty! thou art,
For there thy habitation is the heart—
The heart which love of Thee alone can bind.
And when thy sons to fetters are consign'd,[†]
To fetters, and the damp vault's dayless gloom,
Their country conquers with their martyrdom,
And Freedom's fame finds wings on every wind.[†]
Chillon![†] thy prison is a holy place
And thy sad floor an altar, for 'twas trod,
Until his very steps have left a trace
Worn as if thy cold pavement were a sod,
By Bonnivard![†] May none those marks efface!
For they appeal from tyranny to God.

She Walks in Beauty

She walks in beauty like the night[†]
Of cloudless climes and starry skies,
And all that's best of dark and bright
Meet in her aspect and her eyes;
Thus mellowed to the tender light
Which heaven to gaudy day denies.

One ray the more, one shade the less
Had half impaired[†] the nameless grace
Which waves in every raven tress[†]
Or softly lightens o'er her face,
Where thoughts serenely sweet express
How pure, how dear their dwelling place.

And on that cheek and o'er that brow
So soft, so calm yet eloquent,
The smiles that win, the tints that glow
But tell of days in goodness spent
A mind at peace with all below,
A heart whose love is innocent.

Prometheus

Titan!† to whose immortal eyes
The sufferings of mortality,
Seen in their sad reality,
Were not as things that gods despise;
What was thy pity's recompense?
A silent suffering, and intense;
The rock, the vulture, and the chain,†
All that the proud can feel of pain,
The agony they do not show,
The suffocating sense of woe,
Which speaks but in its loneliness,
And then is jealous lest the sky
Should have a listener, nor will sigh
Until its voice is echoless.

Titan! to thee the strife was given
Between the suffering and the will,
Which torture where they cannot kill;
And the inexorable Heaven,
And the deaf tyranny of Fate,
The ruling principle of Hate,
Which for its pleasure doth create
The things it may annihilate,
Refus'd thee even the boon to die:
The wretched gift Eternity
Was thine—and thou hast borne it well.
All that the Thunderer† wrung from thee
Was but the menace which flung back
On him the torments of thy rack;
The fate thou didst so well foresee,
But would not to appease him tell;
And in thy Silence was his Sentence,
And in his Soul a vain repentance,
And evil dread so ill dissembled,
That in his hand the lightnings trembled.

Thy Godlike crime was to be kind,[†]
To render with thy precepts less
The sum of human wretchedness,
And strengthen Man with his own mind;
But baffled as thou wert from high,
Still in thy patient energy,
In the endurance, and repulse
Of thine impenetrable Spirit,
Which Earth and Heaven could not convulse,
A mighty lesson we inherit:
Thou art a symbol and a sign
To Mortals of their fate and force;
Like thee, Man is in part divine,
A troubled stream from a pure source;
And Man in portions can foresee
His own funereal destiny;
His wretchedness, and his resistance,
And his sad unallied existence:
To which his Spirit may oppose
Itself—and equal to all woes,
And a firm will, and a deep sense,
Which even in torture can descry
Its own concenter'd recompense,
Triumphant where it dares defy,
And making Death a Victory.

PERCY BYSSHE SHELLEY

"Our sweetest songs are those that tell of saddest thought."

— PERCY BYSSHE SHELLEY
"To a Skylark"

PERCY BYSSHE SHELLEY was born on August 4, 1792, near Horsham in Sussex, England, into an aristocratic family. His father was Timothy Shelley, a Sussex squire and a member of Parliament.

In 1810, Shelley entered the Oxford University College only to be expelled the next year for publishing a pamphlet entitled "The Necessity of Atheism," which he wrote with Thomas Jefferson Hogg. After his expulsion, Shelley eloped with Harriet Westbrook, the 16-year-old daughter of a London tavern owner. The scandal of his son's marrying such an inappropriate bride under such questionable circumstances caused Shelley's father to withdraw Shelley's inheritance and replace it with a small allowance. Shelley and Harriet spent the next two years traveling throughout England and Ireland, speaking out for their causes; however, they separated soon afterwards. In 1813, Shelley published his first important poem, *Queen Mab*.

In 1814, Shelley met and eloped with Mary Wollstonecraft Godwin, the daughter of the philosopher and anarchist William Godwin and the feminist Mary Wollstonecraft.

After their return to London, Shelley inherited an annual income from his grandfather's will, and Shelley married Mary.

The Shelleys spent the summer of 1816 with Lord Byron at Lake Geneva, where Shelley composed the "Hymn to Intellectual Beauty" and "Mont Blanc." It was during this time that Mary began writing the story that would become her famous *Frankenstein*.

Shelley published "Ozymandias" in 1818. In the spring of 1821, he wrote *Adonais* for John Keats, who had died in Rome, and whom he admired. The pastoral elegy was first published in July 1821.

In 1822, the Shelley household moved to the Bay of Lerici in Italy. To welcome his visiting friend Leigh Hunt, he sailed to Leghorn (Livorno). During a storm on the return voyage, his small schooner sank, and Shelley drowned, along with Edward Williams, on July 8, 1822. The bodies washed ashore at Viareggio, where they were burned on the beach. Leigh Hunt and Lord Byron witnessed the cremation. Shelley's ashes were later buried in Rome.

Ozymandias †

I met a traveller from an antique land
Who said: Two vast and trunkless legs of stone
Stand in the desert. . . .Near them, on the sand,
Half sunk, a shattered visage lies, whose frown,
And wrinkled lip, and sneer of cold command,
Tell that its sculptor well those passions read
Which yet survive, stamped on these lifeless things,
The hand that mocked them, and the heart that fed:
And on the pedestal these words appear:
'My name is Ozymandias, king of kings:
Look on my works, ye Mighty, and despair!'†
Nothing beside remains. Round the decay
Of that colossal wreck, boundless and bare
The lone and level sands stretch far away.

Ode to the West Wind †

1

O wild West Wind,† thou breath of Autumn's being,
Thou, from whose unseen presence the leaves dead
Are driven, like ghosts from an enchanter fleeing,

Yellow,† and black, and pale, and hectic red,
Pestilence-stricken multitudes: O thou,
Who chariotest to their dark wintry bed

The winged seeds, where they lie cold and low,
Each like a corpse within its grave, until
Thine azure sister of the Spring shall blow

Her clarion o'er the dreaming earth, and fill
(Driving sweet buds like flocks to feed in air)
With living hues and odours plain and hill:

Wild Spirit, which art moving everywhere;
Destroyer and preserver; hear, oh, hear!

2

Thou on whose stream, 'mid the steep sky's commotion,
Loose clouds like earth's decaying leaves are shed,
Shook from the tangled boughs of Heaven and Ocean,

Angels of rain and lightning: there are spread
On the blue surface of thine aery surge,
Like the bright hair uplifted from the head

Of some fierce Mænad,† even from the dim verge
Of the horizon to the zenith's height,
The locks of the approaching storm. Thou Dirge

Of the dying year, to which this closing night
Will be the dome of a vast sepulchre,
Vaulted with all thy congregated might

Of vapours, from whose solid atmosphere
Black rain, and fire, and hail will burst: oh, hear!

3

Thou who didst waken from his summer dreams
The blue Mediterranean, where he lay,
Lulled by the coil of his crystalline streams,

Beside a pumice isle in Baiae's bay,[†]
And saw in sleep old palaces and towers
Quivering within the wave's intenser day,

All overgrown with azure moss and flowers
So sweet, the sense faints picturing them! Thou
For whose path the Atlantic's level powers

Cleave themselves into chasms, while far below
The sea-blooms and the oozy woods which wear
The sapless foliage of the ocean, know

Thy voice, and suddenly grow gray with fear,
And tremble and despoil themselves: oh, hear!

4

If I were a dead leaf thou mightest bear;
If I were a swift cloud to fly with thee;
A wave to pant beneath thy power, and share

The impulse of thy strength, only less free
Than thou, O uncontrollable! If even
I were as in my boyhood, and could be

The comrade of thy wanderings over Heaven,
As then, when to outstrip thy skiey speed
Scarce seemed a vision; I would ne'er have striven

As thus with thee in prayer in my sore need.
Oh, lift me as a wave, a leaf, a cloud!
I fall upon the thorns of life! I bleed!

A heavy weight of hours has chained and bowed
One too like thee: tameless, and swift, and proud.

5

Make me thy lyre, even as the forest is:
What if my leaves are falling like its own!
The tumult of thy mighty harmonies

Will take from both a deep, autumnal tone,
Sweet though in sadness. Be thou, Spirit fierce,
My spirit! Be thou me, impetuous one!

Drive my dead thoughts over the universe
Like withered leaves to quicken a new birth!
And, by the incantation of this verse,

Scatter, as from an unextinguished hearth
Ashes and sparks, my words among mankind!
Be through my lips to unawakened earth

The trumpet of a prophecy! O, Wind,
If Winter comes, can Spring be far behind?

Adonais †

1

I weep for Adonais—he is dead!
Oh weep for Adonais, though our tears
Thaw not the frost which binds so dear a head!
And thou, sad Hour selected from all years
To mourn our loss, rouse thy obscure compeers,
And teach them thine own sorrow! Say: 'With me
Died Adonais! Till the future dares
Forget the past, his fate and fame shall be
An echo and a light unto eternity.'

2

Where wert thou, mighty Mother,† when he lay,
When thy son lay, pierced by the shaft which flies
In darkness? Where was lorn Urania†
When Adonais died? With veiléd eyes,
'Mid listening Echoes, in her paradise
She sate, while one, with soft enamoured breath,
Rekindled all the fading melodies
With which, like flowers that mock the corse beneath,
He had adorned and hid the coming bulk of Death.

3

Oh weep for Adonais—he is dead!
Wake, melancholy Mother, wake and weep!—
Yet wherefore? Quench within their burning bed
Thy fiery tears, and let thy loud heart keep,
Like his, a mute and uncomplaining sleep;
For he is gone where all things wise and fair
Descend. Oh dream not that the amorous deep
Will yet restore him to the vital air;
Death feeds on his mute voice, and laughs at our despair.

4

Most musical of mourners, weep again!
Lament anew, Urania!—He died[†]
Who was the sire of an immortal strain,
Blind, old, and lonely, when his country's pride
The priest, the slave, and the liberticide,
Trampled and mocked with many a loathéd rite
Of lust and blood. He went unterrified
Into the gulf of death; but his clear sprite
Yet reigns o'er earth, the third among the Sons of Light.[†]

5

Most musical of mourners, weep anew!
Not all to that bright station dared to climb:
And happier they their happiness who knew,
Whose tapers yet burn through that night of time
In which suns perished. Others more sublime,
Struck by the envious wrath of man or God,
Have sunk, extinct in their refulgent prime;
And some yet live, treading the thorny road
Which leads, through toil and hate, to Fame's serene abode.

6

But now thy youngest, dearest one has perished,[†]
The nursling of thy widowhood, who grew,
Like a pale flower by some sad maiden cherished,
And fed with true love tears instead of dew.
Most musical of mourners, weep anew!
Thy extreme hope, the loveliest and the last,
The bloom whose petals, nipt before they blew,
Died on the promise of the fruit, is waste;
The broken lily lies—the storm is overpast.

7

To that high Capital where kingly Death
Keeps his pale court in beauty and decay
He came; and bought, with price of purest breath,
A grave among the eternal.—Come away!
Haste, while the vault of blue Italian day
Is yet his fitting charnel-roof, while still
He lies as if in dewy sleep he lay.
Awake him not! surely he takes his fill
Of deep and liquid rest, forgetful of all ill.

8

He will awake no more, oh never more!
Within the twilight chamber spreads apace
The shadow of white Death, and at the door
Invisible Corruption waits to trace
His extreme way to her dim dwelling-place;
The eternal Hunger sits, but pity and awe
Soothe her pale rage, nor dares she to deface
So fair a prey, till darkness and the law
Of change shall o'er his sleep the mortal curtain draw.

9

Oh weep for Adonais!—The quick Dreams,
The passion-wingéd ministers of thought,
Who were his flocks, whom near the living streams
Of his young spirit he fed, and whom he taught
The love which was its music, wander not—
Wander no more from kindling brain to brain,
But droop there whence they sprung; and mourn their lot
Round the cold heart where, after their sweet pain,
They ne'er will gather strength or find a home again.

10

And one with trembling hands clasps his cold head,
And fans him with her moonlight wings, and cries,
'Our love, our hope, our sorrow, is not dead!
See, on the silken fringe of his faint eyes,
Like dew upon a sleeping flower, there lies
A tear some Dream has loosened from his brain,'
Lost angel of a ruined paradise!
She knew not 'twas her own,—as with no stain
She faded, like a cloud which had outwept its rain.

11

One from a lucid urn of starry dew
Washed his light limbs, as if embalming them;
Another dipt her profuse locks, and threw
The wreath upon him, like an anadem
Which frozen tears instead of pearls begem;
Another in her wilful grief would break
Her bow and wingéd reeds, as if to stem
A greater loss with one which was more weak,
And dull the barbéd fire against his frozen cheek.

12

Another Splendour on his mouth alit,
That mouth whence it was wont to draw the breath
Which gave it strength to pierce the guarded wit,
And pass into the panting heart beneath
With lightning and with music: the damp death
Quenched its caress upon his icy lips;
And, as a dying meteor stains a wreath
Of moonlight vapour which the cold night clips,
It flushed through his pale limbs, and passed to its eclipse.

13

And others came,—Desires and Adorations,
Wingéd Persuasions, and veiled Destinies,
Splendours, and Glooms, and glimmering incarnations
Of Hopes and Fears, and twilight Phantasies;
And Sorrow, with her family of Sighs,
And Pleasure, blind with tears, led by the gleam
Of her own dying smile instead of eyes,
Came in slow pomp;—the moving pomp might seem
Like pageantry of mist on an autumnal stream.

14

All he had loved, and moulded into thought
From shape and hue and odour and sweet sound.
Lamented Adonais. Morning sought
Her eastern watch-tower, and her hair unbound,
Wet with the tears which should adorn the ground,
Dimmed the aerial eyes that kindle day;
Afar the melancholy Thunder moaned,
Pale Ocean in unquiet slumber lay,
And the wild Winds flew round, sobbing in their dismay.

15

Lost Echo sits amid the voiceless mountains,
And feeds her grief with his remembered lay,
And will no more reply to winds or fountains,
Or amorous birds perched on the young green spray,
Or herdsman's horn, or bell at closing day;
Since she can mimic not his lips, more dear
Than those for whose disdain she pined away
Into a shadow of all sounds:—a drear
Murmur, between their songs, is all the woodmen hear.

16

Grief made the young Spring wild, and she threw down
Her kindling buds, as if she Autumn were,
Or they dead leaves; since her delight is flown,
For whom should she have waked the sullen Year?
To Phoebus was not Hyacinth so dear,†
Nor to himself Narcissus,† as to both
Thou, Adonais; wan they stand and sere
Amid the faint companions of their youth,
With dew all turned to tears,—odour, to sighing ruth.

17

Thy spirit's sister, the lorn nightingale,
Mourns not her mate with such melodious pain;
Not so the eagle, who like thee could scale
Heaven, and could nourish in the sun's domain
Her mighty young with morning, doth complain,
Soaring and screaming round her empty nest,
As Albion† wails for thee: the curse of Cain†
Light on his head who pierced thy innocent breast,
And scared the angel soul that was its earthly guest!

18

Ah woe is me! Winter is come and gone,
But grief returns with the revolving year.
The airs and streams renew their joyous tone;
The ants, the bees, the swallows, re-appear;
Fresh leaves and flowers deck the dead Seasons' bier;
The amorous birds now pair in every brake,
And build their mossy homes in field and brere;
And the green lizard and the golden snake,
Like unimprisoned flames, out of their trance awake.

19

Through wood and stream and field and hill and ocean,
A quickening life from the Earth's heart has burst,
As it has ever done, with change and motion,
From the great morning of the world when first
God dawned on chaos. In its steam immersed,
The lamps of heaven flash with a softer light;
All baser things pant with life's sacred thirst,
Diffuse themselves, and spend in love's delight
The beauty and the joy of their renewéd might.

20

The leprous corpse, touched by this spirit tender,
Exhales itself in flowers of gentle breath;
Like incarnations of the stars, when splendour
Is changed to fragrance, they illumine death,
And mock the merry worm that wakes beneath.
Nought we know dies: shall that alone which knows
Be as a sword consumed before the sheath
By sightless lightning? Th' intense atom glows
A moment, then is quenched in a most cold repose.

21

Alas that all we loved of him should be,
But for our grief, as if it had not been,
And grief itself be mortal! Woe is me!
Whence are we, and why are we? of what scene
The actors or spectators? Great and mean
Meet massed in death, who lends what life must borrow.
As long as skies are blue and fields are green,
Evening must usher night, night urge the morrow,
Month follow month with woe, and year wake year to sorrow.

22

He will awake no more, oh never more!
'Wake thou,' cried Misery, 'childless Mother; Rise
Out of thy sleep, and slake in thy heart's core
A wound more fierce than his, with tears and sighs.'
And all the Dreams that watched Urania's eyes,
And all the Echoes whom their Sister's song
Had held in holy silence, cried 'Arise!'
Swift as a thought by the snake memory stung,
From her ambrosial[†] rest the fading Splendour sprung.

23

She rose like an autumnal Night that springs
Out of the east, and follows wild and drear
The golden Day, which on eternal wings,
Even as a ghost abandoning a bier,
Had left the Earth a corpse. Sorrow and fear
So struck, so roused, so rapt, Urania;
So saddened round her like an atmosphere
Of stormy mist; so swept her on her way,
Even to the mournful place where Adonais lay.

24

Out of her secret paradise she sped,
Through camps and cities rough with stone and steel
And human hearts, which, to her aery tread
Yielding not, wounded the invisible
Palms of her tender feet where'er they fell.
And barbéd tongues, and thoughts more sharp than they,
Rent the soft form they never could repel,
Whose sacred blood, like the young tears of May,
Paved with eternal flowers that undeserving way.

25

In the death-chamber for a moment Death,
Shamed by the presence of that living might,
Blushed to annihilation, and the breath
Revisited those lips, and life's pale light
Flashed through those limbs so late her dear delight.
'Leave me not wild and drear and comfortless,
As silent lightning leaves the starless night!
Leave me not!' cried Urania. Her distress
Roused Death: Death rose and smiled, and met her vain caress.

26

'Stay yet awhile! speak to me once again!
Kiss me, so long but as a kiss may live!
And in my heartless breast and burning brain
That word, that kiss, shall all thoughts else survive,
With food of saddest memory kept alive,
Now thou art dead, as if it were a part
Of thee, my Adonais! I would give
All that I am, to be as thou now art:—
But I am chained to Time, and cannot thence depart.

27

'O gentle child, beautiful as thou wert,
Why didst thou leave the trodden paths of men
Too soon, and with weak hands though mighty heart
Dare the unpastured dragon in his den?
Defenceless as thou wert, oh where was then
Wisdom the mirrored shield, or scorn the spear?—
Or, hadst thou waited the full cycle when
Thy spirit should have filled its crescent sphere,
The monsters of life's waste had fled from thee like deer.

28

'The herded wolves bold only to pursue,
The obscene ravens clamorous o'er the dead,
The vultures[†] to the conqueror's banner true,
Who feed where desolation first has fed,
And whose wings rain contagion,—how they fled,
When like Apollo,[†] from his golden bow,
The Pythian[†] of the age one arrow sped,
And smiled!—The spoilers tempt no second blow,
They fawn on the proud feet that spurn them lying low.

29

'The sun comes forth, and many reptiles spawn:
He sets, and each ephemeral insect then
Is gathered into death without a dawn,
And the immortal stars awake again.
So is it in the world of living men:
A godlike mind soars forth, in its delight
Making earth bare and veiling heaven; and, when
It sinks, the swarms that dimmed or shared its light
Leave to its kindred lamps the spirit's awful night.'

30

Thus ceased she: and the Mountain Shepherds came,
Their garlands sere, their magic mantles rent.
The Pilgrim of Eternity,[†] whose fame
Over his living head like heaven is bent,
An early but enduring monument,
Came, veiling all the lightnings of his song
In sorrow. From her wilds Ierne sent
The sweetest lyrist of her saddest wrong,[†]
And love taught grief to fall like music from his tongue.

31

'Midst others of less note came one frail form,
A phantom among men, companionless[†]
As the last cloud of an expiring storm
Whose thunder is its knell. He, as I guess,
Had gazed on Nature's naked loveliness
Actaeon[†]-like; and now he fled astray
With feeble steps o'er the world's wilderness,
And his own thoughts along that rugged way
Pursued like raging hounds their father and their prey.

32

A pard-like Spirit beautiful and swift—
A love in desolation masked—a power
Girt round with weakness; it can scarce uplift
The weight of the superincumbent hour.
It is a dying lamp, a falling shower,
A breaking billow;—even whilst we speak
Is it not broken? On the withering flower
The killing sun smiles brightly: on a cheek
The life can burn in blood even while the heart may break.

33

His head was bound with pansies overblown,
And faded violets, white and pied and blue;
And a light spear topped with a cypress cone,
Round whose rude shaft dark ivy tresses grew
Yet dripping with the forest's noonday dew,
Vibrated, as the ever-beating heart
Shook the weak hand that grasped it. Of that crew
He came the last, neglected and apart;
A herd-abandoned deer struck by the hunter's dart.

34

All stood aloof, and at his partial moan
Smiled through their tears; well knew that gentle band
Who in another's fate now wept his own;
As in the accents of an unknown land
He sang new sorrow; sad Urania scanned
The Stranger's mien and murmured 'Who art thou?'
He answered not, but with a sudden hand
Made bare his branded and ensanguined brow,
Which was like Cain's or Christ's—Oh that it should be so!

35

What softer voice is hushed over the dead?
Athwart what brow is that dark mantle thrown?
What form leans sadly o'er the white death-bed,
In mockery of monumental stone,
The heavy heart heaving without a moan?
If it be he who, gentlest of the wise,
Taught, soothed, loved, honoured, the departed one.
Let me not vex with inharmonious sighs
The silence of that heart's accepted sacrifice.

36

Our Adonais has drunk poison—oh
What deaf and viperous murderer could crown
Life's early cup with such a draught of woe?
The nameless worm would now itself disown;
It felt, yet could escape, the magic tone
Whose prelude held all envy, hate, and wrong,
But what was howling in one breast alone,
Silent with expectation of the song
Whose master's hand is cold, whose silver lyre unstrung.

37

Live thou, whose infamy is not thy fame!
Live! fear no heavier chastisement from me,
Thou noteless blot on a remembered name!
But be thyself, and know thyself to be!
And ever at thy season be thou free
To spill the venom when thy fangs o'erflow;
Remorse and self-contempt shall cling to thee,
Hot shame shall burn upon thy secret brow,
And like a beaten hound tremble thou shalt—as now.

38

Nor let us weep that our delight is fled
Far from these carrion kites that scream below.
He wakes or sleeps with the enduring dead;
Thou canst not soar where he is sitting now.
Dust to the dust: but the pure spirit shall flow
Back to the burning fountain whence it came,
A portion of the Eternal, which must glow
Through time and change, unquenchably the same,
Whilst thy cold embers choke the sordid hearth of shame.

39

Peace, peace! he is not dead, he doth not sleep!
He hath awakened from the dream of life.
'Tis we who, lost in stormy visions, keep
With phantoms an unprofitable strife,
And in mad trance strike with our spirit's knife
Invulnerable nothings. We decay
Like corpses in a charnel; fear and grief
Convulse us and consume us day by day,
And cold hopes swarm like worms within our living clay.

40

He has outsoared the shadow of our night.
Envy and calumny and hate and pain,
And that unrest which men miscall delight,
Can touch him not and torture not again.
From the contagion of the world's slow stain
He is secure; and now can never mourn
A heart grown cold, a head grown grey in vain—
Nor, when the spirit's self has ceased to burn,
With sparkless ashes load an unlamented urn.

41

He lives, he wakes—'tis Death is dead, not he;
Mourn not for Adonais.—Thou young Dawn,
Turn all thy dew to splendour, for from thee
The spirit thou lamentest is not gone!
Ye caverns and ye forests, cease to moan!
Cease, ye faint flowers and fountains! and thou Air,
Which like a mourning veil thy scarf hadst thrown
O'er the abandoned Earth, now leave it bare
Even to the joyous stars which smile on its despair!

42

He is made one with Nature. There is heard
His voice in all her music, from the moan
Of thunder to the song of night's sweet bird.
He is a presence to be felt and known
In darkness and in light, from herb and stone,
Spreading itself where'er that Power may move
Which has withdrawn his being to its own,
Which wields the world with never wearied love,
Sustains it from beneath, and kindles it above.

43

He is a portion of the loveliness
Which once he made more lovely. He doth bear
His part, while the One Spirit's plastic stress
Sweeps through the dull dense world; compelling there
All new successions to the forms they wear;
Torturing th' unwilling dross, that checks its flight,
To its own likeness, as each mass may bear;
And bursting in its beauty and its might
From trees and beasts and men into the heaven's light.

44

The splendours of the firmament of time
May be eclipsed, but are extinguished not;
Like stars to their appointed height they climb,
And death is a low mist which cannot blot
The brightness it may veil. When lofty thought
Lifts a young heart above its mortal lair,
And love and life contend in it for what
Shall be its earthly doom, the dead live there,
And move like winds of light on dark and stormy air.

45

The inheritors of unfulfilled renown
Rose from their thrones, built beyond mortal thought,
Far in the unapparent. Chatterton†
Rose pale, his solemn agony had not
Yet faded from him; Sidney,† as he fought
And as he fell and as he lived and loved
Sublimely mild, a spirit without spot,
Arose; and Lucan,† by his death approved;—
Oblivion as they rose shrank like a thing reproved.

46

And many more, whose names on earth are dark
But whose transmitted effluence cannot die
So long as fire outlives the parent spark,
Rose, robed in dazzling immortality.
'Thou art become as one of us,' they cry;
'It was for thee yon kingless sphere has long
Swung blind in unascended majesty,
Silent alone amid an heaven of song.
Assume thy wingéd throne, thou Vesper of our throng!'

47

Who mourns for Adonais? Oh come forth,
Fond wretch, and know thyself and him aright.
Clasp with thy panting soul the pendulous earth;
As from a centre, dart thy spirit's light
Beyond all worlds, until its spacious might
Satiate the void circumference: then shrink
Even to a point within our day and night;
And keep thy heart light lest it make thee sink
When hope has kindled hope, and lured thee to the brink.

48

Or go to Rome, which is the sepulchre,
Oh not of him, but of our joy. 'Tis nought
That ages, empires, and religions, there
Lie buried in the ravage they have wrought;
For such as he can lend—they borrow not
Glory from those who made the world their prey:
And he is gathered to the kings of thought
Who waged contention with their time's decay,
And of the past are all that cannot pass away.

49

Go thou to Rome,—at once the paradise,
The grave, the city, and the wilderness;
And where its wrecks like shattered mountains rise,
And flowering weeds and fragrant copses dress
The bones of Desolation's nakedness,
Pass, till the Spirit of the spot shall lead
Thy footsteps to a slope of green access,
Where, like an infant's smile, over the dead
A light of laughing flowers along the grass is spread.

50

And grey walls moulder round, on which dull Time
Feeds, like slow fire upon a hoary brand;
And one keen pyramid with wedge sublime,
Pavilioning the dust of him who planned
This refuge for his memory, doth stand
Like flame transformed to marble; and beneath
A field is spread, on which a newer band
Have pitched in heaven's smile their camp of death,
Welcoming him we lose with scarce extinguished breath.

51

Here pause. These graves are all too young as yet
To have outgrown the sorrow which consigned
Its charge to each; and, if the seal is set
Here on one fountain of a mourning mind,
Break it not thou! too surely shalt thou find
Thine own well full, if thou returnest home,
Of tears and gall. From the world's bitter wind
Seek shelter in the shadow of the tomb.
What Adonais is why fear we to become?

52

The One remains, the many change and pass;
Heaven's light for ever shines, earth's shadows fly;
Life, like a dome of many-coloured glass,
Stains the white radiance of eternity,
Until Death tramples it to fragments.—Die,
If thou wouldst be with that which thou dost seek!
Follow where all is fled!—Rome's azure sky,
Flowers, ruins, statues, music, words, are weak
The glory they transfuse with fitting truth to speak.

53

Why linger, why turn back, why shrink, my heart?
Thy hopes are gone before: from all things here
They have departed; thou shouldst now depart!
A light is past from the revolving year,
And man and woman; and what still is dear
Attracts to crush, repels to make thee wither.
The soft sky smiles, the low wind whispers near:
'Tis Adonais calls! Oh hasten thither!
No more let life divide what death can join together.

54

That light whose smile kindles the universe,
That beauty in which all things work and move,
That benediction which the eclipsing curse
Of birth can quench not, that sustaining Love
Which, through the web of being blindly wove
By man and beast and earth and air and sea,
Burns bright or dim, as each are mirrors of
The fire for which all thirst, now beams on me,
Consuming the last clouds of cold mortality.

55

The breath whose might I have invoked in song
Descends on me; my spirit's bark is driven
Far from the shore, far from the trembling throng
Whose sails were never to the tempest given.
The massy earth and spheréd skies are riven!
I am borne darkly, fearfully, afar!
Whilst, burning through the inmost veil of heaven,
The soul of Adonais, like a star,
Beacons from the abode where the Eternal are.

JOHN KEATS

A thing of beauty is a joy forever:
Its loveliness increases; it will never
Pass into nothingness.

—JOHN KEATS
Endymion

JOHN KEATS was born in London on October 31, 1795, to a prosperous livery-stable manager. John was the oldest of five children (one died in infancy), who remained deeply devoted to each other. Only a few months after their father died of a fractured skull in 1804, Keats's mother remarried. Almost as quickly, she left her second husband and the prosperous business she had inherited from Keats's father. She moved with the children to live with her mother at Edmonton, near London; however, she died of tuberculosis in 1810, leaving the children in the care of their grandmother.

At school, Keats and his brothers were popular. Keats read widely and avidly. His first poem, "Lines in Imitation of Spenser," was written in 1814. He moved to London in 1815 to study surgery at Guy's Hospital. Before leaving his medical career to devote himself exclusively to his poetry, Keats also worked as a junior house surgeon. While in London, he met Leigh Hunt, the editor of *The Examiner*, who introduced him to other young

Romantic poets, including Shelley. Keats's poem, "O Solitude," appeared in *The Examiner*.

Keats's first book, *Poems*, was published in 1817. "Endymion," his first long poem, appeared when he was 21. Keats's greatest works were written in the late 1810s: "Lamia," "The Eve of St. Agnes," and the great odes: "Ode to a Nightingale," "Ode To Autumn," and "Ode on a Grecian Urn." For a short time, he wrote for *The Champion* as a theatrical critic.

Keats spent three months in 1818 caring for his brother Tom, who died of tuberculosis in December.

In 1820, the second volume of Keats's poems was published to considerable critical acclaim. Keats had, however, already diagnosed his own tuberculosis, and his poems reflect his deep sorrow at being unable to marry Fanny Brawne, the woman he loved.

Percy Shelley invited Keats to join him at Pisa, in Italy, but Keats went to Rome instead, believing the climate would be good for his health; he died there on February 23, 1821, at the age of 25.

Keats had already dictated the epitaph he wanted carved on his headstone: "Here lies one whose name was writ in water."

To Hope

When by my solitary hearth I sit,
    And hateful thoughts enwrap my soul in gloom;
When no fair dreams before my "mind's eye" flit,
    And the bare heath of life presents no bloom;
    Sweet Hope, ethereal balm upon me shed,
    And wave thy silver pinions o'er my head.

Whene'er I wander, at the fall of night,
    Where woven boughs shut out the moon's bright ray,
Should sad Despondency my musings fright,
    And frown, to drive fair Cheerfulness away,
    Peep with the moon-beams through the leafy roof,
    And keep that fiend Despondence far aloof.

Should Disappointment, parent of Despair,
    Strive for her son to seize my careless heart;
When, like a cloud, he sits upon the air,
    Preparing on his spell-bound prey to dart:
    Chase him away, sweet Hope, with visage bright,
    And fright him as the morning frightens night!

Whene'er the fate of those I hold most dear
    Tells to my fearful breast a tale of sorrow,
O bright-eyed Hope, my morbid fancy cheer;
    Let me awhile thy sweetest comforts borrow:
    Thy heaven-born radiance around me shed,
    And wave thy silver pinions o'er my head!

Should e'er unhappy love my bosom pain,
    From cruel parents, or relentless fair;
O let me think it is not quite in vain
    To sigh out sonnets to the midnight air!
    Sweet Hope, ethereal balm upon me shed.
    And wave thy silver pinions o'er my head!

In the long vista of the years to roll,
    Let me not see our country's honour fade:
O let me see our land retain her soul,
    Her pride, her freedom; and not freedom's shade.
    From thy bright eyes unusual brightness shed—
    Beneath thy pinions canopy my head!

Let me not see the patriot's high bequest,
    Great Liberty! how great in plain attire!
With the base purple of a court oppress'd,
    Bowing her head, and ready to expire:
    But let me see thee stoop from heaven on wings
    That fill the skies with silver glitterings!

And as, in sparkling majesty, a star
    Gilds the bright summit of some gloomy cloud;
Brightening the half veil'd face of heaven afar:
    So, when dark thoughts my boding spirit shroud,
    Sweet Hope, celestial influence round me shed,
    Waving thy silver pinions o'er my head.

Ode on Melancholy

I.

No, no, go not to Lethe,† neither twist
Wolf's-bane, tight-rooted, for its poisonous wine;
Nor suffer thy pale forehead to be kiss'd
By nightshade, ruby grape of Proserpine;†
Make not your rosary of yew-berries,
Nor let the beetle, nor the death-moth be
Your mournful Psyche,† nor the downy owl
A partner in your sorrow's mysteries;
For shade to shade will come too drowsily,
And drown the wakeful anguish of the soul.

II.

But when the melancholy fit shall fall
Sudden from heaven like a weeping cloud,
That fosters the droop-headed flowers all,
And hides the green hill in an April shroud;
Then glut thy sorrow on a morning rose,
Or on the rainbow of the salt sand-wave,
Or on the wealth of globed peonies;
Or if thy mistress some rich anger shows,
Emprison her soft hand, and let her rave,
And feed deep, deep upon her peerless eyes.

III.

She dwells with Beauty—Beauty that must die;
And Joy, whose hand is ever at his lips
Bidding adieu; and aching Pleasure nigh,
Turning to Poison while the bee-mouth sips:
Ay, in the very temple of delight
Veil'd Melancholy has her sovran shrine,
Though seen of none save him whose strenuous tongue
Can burst Joy's grape against his palate fine;
His soul shall taste the sadness of her might,
And be among her cloudy trophies hung.

Ode to a Nightingale

My heart aches, and a drowsy numbness pains
  My sense, as though of hemlock[†] I had drunk,
Or emptied some dull opiate to the drains
  One minute past, and Lethe-wards[†] had sunk:
'Tis not through envy of thy happy lot,
  But being too happy in thine happiness—
    That thou, light-wingéd Dryad[†] of the trees,
     In some melodious plot
    Of beechen green, and shadows numberless,
    Singest of summer in full-throated ease.

O, for a draught of vintage! that hath been
  Cool'd a long age in the deep-delvéd earth,
Tasting of Flora and the country green,
  Dance, and Provencal song, and sunburnt mirth!
O for a beaker full of the warm south,
  Full of the true, the blushful Hippocrene,[†]
    With beaded bubbles winking at the brim,
    And purple-stainèd mouth;
    That I might drink, and leave the world unseen,
    And with thee fade away into the forest dim—

Fade far away, dissolve, and quite forget
  What thou among the leaves hast never known,
The weariness, the fever, and the fret
  Here, where men sit and hear each other groan;
Where palsy shakes a few, sad, last gray hairs,
  Where youth grows pale, and spectre-thin, and dies;
    Where but to think is to be full of sorrow
    And leaden-eyed despairs,
    Where Beauty cannot keep her lustrous eyes,
    Or new Love pine at them beyond to-morrow.

Away! away! for I will fly to thee,
  Not charioted by Bacchus[†] and his pards,
But on the viewless wings of Poesy,
  Though the dull brain perplexes and retards.
Already with thee! tender is the night,
  And haply the Queen-Moon is on her throne,
    Cluster'd around by all her starry Fays;
      But here there is no light,
  Save what from heaven is with the breezes blown
    Through verdurous glooms and winding mossy ways.

I cannot see what flowers are at my feet,
  Nor what soft incense hangs upon the boughs,
But, in embalmèd darkness, guess each sweet
  Wherewith the seasonable month endows
The grass, the thicket, and the fruit-tree wild;
  White hawthorn, and the pastoral eglantine;
    Fast fading violets cover'd up in leaves;
      And mid-May's eldest child,
  The coming musk-rose, full of dewy wine,
    The murmurous haunt of flies on summer eves.

Darkling I listen; and, for many a time
  I have been half in love with easeful Death,
Call'd him soft names in many a musèd rhyme,
  To take into the air my quiet breath;
Now more than ever seems it rich to die,
  To cease upon the midnight with no pain,
    While thou art pouring forth thy soul abroad
      In such an ecstasy!
  Still wouldst thou sing, and I have ears in vain—
    To thy high requiem become a sod.

Thou wast not born for death, immortal Bird!
  No hungry generations tread thee down;
The voice I hear this passing night was heard
  In ancient days by emperor and clown:
Perhaps the self-same song that found a path
  Through the sad heart of Ruth,[†] when, sick for home,
    She stood in tears amid the alien corn;
      The same that oft-times hath
  Charm'd magic casements, opening on the foam
    Of perilous seas, in faery lands forlorn.

Forlorn! the very word is like a bell
  To toll me back from thee to my sole self!
Adieu! the fancy cannot cheat so well
  As she is fam'd to do, deceiving elf.
Adieu! adieu! thy plaintive anthem fades
    Past the near meadows, over the still stream,
      Up the hill-side; and now 'tis buried deep
        In the next valley-glades:
    Was it a vision, or a waking dream?
    Fled is that music—Do I wake or sleep?

Glossary

THE RIME OF THE ANCIENT MARINER IN SEVEN PARTS

Lyrical Ballads – the major work on which Coleridge and Wordsworth collaborated; its publication is usually credited with ushering in the Romantic Era.

"Facile credo, plures... *Archaeol. Phil.*, p. 68" – [*Latin*] I well believe there to be more unseen natural things than visible in the universe of things. But who will explain to us all the families of these things? And the ranks and the relations and differentiating traits and the roles of each of them? What do they do? In what places do they live? Human knowledge has always circled around an understanding of such matters, but has never touched it. It helps, meanwhile, I do not deny, to consider in the mind, just as upon a tablet, the picture of a bigger and better world: that no mind accustomed to the minutia of today's life might draw itself together too much, and totally sink down into unimportant meditations. But meanwhile, one should be devoted to the truth, and order should be preserved, that we may distinguish certain from uncertain and day from night.

the Line – the equator; the imaginary line on the earth that separates the Northern and Southern Hemispheres

PART THE FIRST.

"Till over the mast at noon" – Be careful to note when the Mariner has stopped speaking and the narrator begins.

Albatross – a large sea bird; before the publication of this poem, there was no superstition about killing albatrosses, and they were often killed as food for the sailors. There was, however, some belief that an albatross was the reincarnated soul of a sailor lost at sea.

vespers nine – a religious service; evening prayers performed at nine o'clock; readers should note that Coleridge uses the number nine at least three times in this poem.

PART THE SECOND.

"As idle as a painted ship / Upon a painted ocean." – This is one of the most famous similes and images in English literature. The couplet that follows about there being nothing to drink while surrounded by vast amounts of water is also quite famous.

"...Of the spirit...the land of mist and snow." – The spirit of the slain albatross is "swimming" nine fathoms beneath the ship and has done so since the Mariner killed it somewhere near the South Pole. A fathom is equal to six feet.

"Instead of the Cross, the Albatross / About my neck was hung." – This act is the source of the common expression "having an albatross around [one's] neck," meaning a burden or a curse that weighs someone down.

PART THE THIRD.

"I bit my arm, I sucked the blood, / And cried, A sail! a sail!" – The Mariner sees a ship, but because there is no water to drink, he must drink his own blood in order to call out to his fellow sailors.

"And straight the Sun...burning face." – This describes the image of the ship's masts silhouetted against the sun.

gossameres – films of cobweb-like material suspended in the air; this suggests how tattered and threadbare the Ghost Ship's sails were.

Her lips – The "female" member of the Ghost Ship's crew is similar to a demon.

naked hulk – the bare, stripped Ghost Ship

casting dice – tossing dice, as if to emphasize that fate is a matter of chance, both that of the Mariner and of the Ghost Ship

thrice – three times; pay attention to the many times Coleridge uses the numbers seven and three and multiples of three, especially nine.

"...They dropped down one by one." – The members of the Mariner's crew die, one by one, each cursing the Mariner with a dying look.

"...Like the whiz of my cross-bow!" – The souls of the dying crew members fly from their bodies with a whirring sound like an arrow leaving a cross-bow. Remember that the Mariner shot the albatross with his cross-bow.

PART THE FOURTH.

"I fear thee, ancient Mariner!" – The Wedding-Guest is speaking again.

"This body dropt not down." – The Wedding-Guest fears that the Mariner is a ghost, but the old man is not. The Mariner did not die when the others did.

"The cold sweat...passed away." – The bodies of the dead crew members, which do not decay, continue to stare at the Mariner with the same expressions and cursing of him that they had before they died.

"...And I blessed them unaware." – The Mariner sees glowing sea life and feels appreciative of living things. When he "blesses" them, the albatross falls off his neck. This act begins the Mariner's redemption.

PART THE FIFTH.

Mary Queen – Mary, the mother of Jesus; in the Catholic faith, she is called "The Queen of Heaven."

"They groaned...dead men rise." – The bodies of the dead crew come "alive" and work the ship.

"Under the keel...made the ship to go." – The spirit of the slain albatross, nine fathoms down, is making the ship move.

"By him who died on cross..." – The one voice is swearing by Jesus.

PART THE SIXTH.

charnel-dungeon fitter – This phrase indicates that the dead men looked as if they were in a morgue-like [*charnel*] dungeon, all dressed in rags and shreds of clothing [*fitter*].

"...by the holy rood!" – The "holy rood" is the cross; the Mariner, therefore, is swearing by the cross.

seraph-man – a seraph, a class of angel

Hermit good – See *hermit's cave* in the "Tintern Abbey" glossary.

PART THE SEVENTH.

" 'Strange, by my faith!' the Hermit said" – The quotation here indicates a dialogue between the hermit and the pilot of the boat.

"Forthwith this frame...within me burns." – The Mariner feels a physical agony that can be cured only by telling his tale.

"He went...the morrow morn." – Both the Mariner and the Wedding-Guest have been healed by the story.

KUBLA KHAN OR A VISION IN A DREAM. A FRAGMENT.

A Fragment. – There is considerable debate over whether this is indeed an incomplete poem and whether it was conceived, as Coleridge is said to have claimed, while he was under the influence of opium.

Xanadu – a mythical city hidden in a secret valley somewhere in the Himalayas

Kubla Khan – the Mongolian conqueror whose empire stretched from European Russia to the eastern shores of China; he was the grandson of Genghis Khan.

Alph – a supposedly underground river, symbolic of a secret or forbidden body of knowledge

thresher's flail – a tool used by a "thresher" to separate the useable and waste parts of the grain

Abyssinian – Ethiopian; the biblical Queen of Sheba came from a region of what is now Ethiopia in Northern Africa.

Mount Abora – possibly an allusion to the Abyssinian legend of the hill Amara, a hill in Ethiopia, used as a prison for the sons of Abyssinian kings; its level top is surrounded by a high wall and is an Eden-like garden of delight.

"And drunk the milk of Paradise." – Here, Coleridge is describing the "madness" of the person who has had the transcendent experience, the vision of Reality, that was desired by the Romantics.

THE LAMB: FROM *SONGS OF INNOCENCE*

Songs of Innocence – one of a pair of companion books Blake wrote looking at issues from two opposing viewpoints

"He is called by thy name." – a reference to Jesus, who is often called "the lamb of God"

"He became a little child." – "The lamb of God" became a child in the form of baby Jesus.

"I a child, & thou a lamb…" – In nursery-rhyme fashion, the speaker identifies with the lamb and with the gentle figure of baby Jesus, the "lamb of God."

THE TYGER: FROM *SONGS OF EXPERIENCE*

Songs of Experience – the companion book to *Songs of Innocence*

"What the hammer?…was thy brain?" – blacksmith imagery associated with the *forging* of the tiger; this is also an allusion to fiery, violent Hell.

"Did He who made the lamb make thee?" – Here the duality of *Innocence* and *Experience* is explicitly revealed. The gentleness of the lamb (innocence) and the fierceness of the tiger (experience) spring from the *same creator.*

THE CHIMNEY SWEEPER: FROM *SONGS OF INNOCENCE*

" 'weep! 'weep! 'weep! 'weep!" – The speaker was so young when he was sold that he could not even say "sweep" properly.

"…head, / That curled…was shaved…" – Prior to advances in modern medicine, it was believed that hair, especially luxurious, curly hair, sapped the strength from the body; therefore, the head was shaved as a means of treating a number of diseases. This could also imply that the child had lice.

their bags – the bags containing their cleaning tools

"So, if all do their duty, they need not fear harm." – This *Songs of Innocence* version ends in a nursery-rhyme type of moral about submitting patiently to suffering, essentially ignoring the apparent horrors of the child chimney-sweepers.

THE CHIMNEY SWEEPER: FROM *SONGS OF EXPERIENCE*

—

A POISON TREE: FROM *SONGS OF EXPERIENCE*

"Till it bore an apple bright…" – probably an allusion to the forbidden fruit (traditionally, but not literally, an apple) eaten by Adam and Eve; this act of disobedience incurred God's wrath and resulted in their being expelled from paradise.

the pole – possibly with the entire heavens, the [poison] tree (on which the apple is growing), or to the North Star, the "pole star" around which the sky seems to rotate; if this is the case, then the night "veiling" the "pole" might indicate a particularly dark, cloudy, or foggy night.

LINES COMPOSED A FEW MILES ABOVE TINTERN ABBEY, ON REVISITING THE BANKS OF THE WYE DURING A TOUR, JULY 13, 1798 FROM *LYRICAL BALLADS*

Wye – a major river in Wales; the ruins of Tintern Abbey stand on its banks.

"These plots of cottage-ground…wild green landscape." – summer; spring is the season of blossoms, and autumn is the season of ripening fruits.

"…as might seem…hermit's cave…" – Note the simile; there is no hermit or hermit's cave, but the smoke rises *like* the smoke from a hermit's cave would. Because of their lives of seclusion in the midst of Nature, hermits represented piety and goodness to the Romantics. They were the "priests" in the religion of nature the Romantics believed in.

"As is a landscape to a blind man's eye…" – The landscape is visible, but a blind man would be unable to perceive it.

"…sensations sweet, / Felt in the blood…" – referring to sensual, emotional feelings, not rational thoughts

no trivial influence – an example of litotes, suggesting that the influence is, indeed, significant

"…that best portion of…kindness and of love." – Rather than some great act of heroism, the best part of this "good man's" life are the little things not even remembered.

"Is lighten'd" – The memory of his previous visit has lightened his mood.

"…we are laid asleep…living soul…" – With the death of the body comes the life of the immortal soul.

"…not only with the sense…For future years." – As the memory of his past visit has brought him joy, so, too, will the memory of this visit bring him joy in the future.

"Not for this…mourn nor murmur…" – He does not complain about the loss of the intense emotional response he once had.

Abundant recompense – He has been paid back *abundantly* for the loss.

thou – Wordsworth's sister, Dorothy

"Thy memory be as…sounds and harmonies…" – The beautiful forms of Nature, when they cannot be seen, still dwell in the memory.

MY HEART LEAPS UP

natural piety – either a devotion to Nature or a devotion that is instinctive and part of one's nature

ODE: INTIMATIONS OF IMMORTALITY FROM RECOLLECTIONS OF EARLY CHILDHOOD

Rainbow – an allusion to "My Heart Leaps Up" and the intense emotional response he had to the sight of beauty in Nature

Shepherd-boy – Because of his youth, and the fact that he lives within the beauty of Nature, the shepherd-boy is similar to a hermit, whom the Romantics idealized as being intimately involved with Nature.

"But there's a Tree…something that is gone…" – Note that this line expresses a similar sentiment to what Wordsworth expresses in "I Travelled Among Unknown Men": a longing for things that are no longer in existence.

visionary gleam – a reference to the "celestial light" of Stanza I that seemed to surround all of Nature

"Our birth is…a forgetting…" – Plato's philosophy states that the Soul has total knowledge, but forgets it in the process of being born into a physical body. Nothing is learned, only remembered.

trailing clouds of glory – Wordsworth differs with Plato, saying that forgetting is not total and abrupt, but gradual.

Shades – Throughout this section, images of darkness will replace images of light as the child grows to adulthood.

light – that "celestial light" of the first stanza and the "visionary gleam," of Stanza IV, whose loss Wordsworth is lamenting

Nature's Priest – The child, closer to the truth, still possesses the "visionary gleam."

vision splendid – another reference to the "celestial light" and "visionary gleam"

"…something of a Mother's mind…" – Earth is not our mother, but acts *like* our mother.

Foster-child – Wordsworth again says that we are not Earth's children, but her foster-children.

Inmate – not only a convict in prison, but any member of a group residing in an institution, like a hospital or boarding school

"Thou, whose exterior…Thy Soul's immensity…" – The child is physically small but has an enormous soul.

"...thou Eye among the blind..." – The child is the one who can still see what the adult has lost sight of.

Perpetual benediction – a never-ending blessing

"...obstinate questionings...outward things..." – the instinct not to accept the *appearance* of things but to look deeper to understand the *essence* of the thing

"...inland far we be...that immortal sea..." – The process of aging and losing the instinctive feelings treasured by the Romantics has been compared to a journey from east to west, from the ocean shore inland.

primal sympathy – the first or earliest feelings of connection with Nature

THE LUCY POEMS

The Lucy Poems – Most of the five "Lucy poems" were written in the winter of 1798-99. The identity of "Lucy" is not known, nor is it known whether "Lucy" is an actual person or merely a fictional/poetic persona.

STRANGE FITS OF PASSION HAVE I KNOWN

fits of passion – intense bursts of emotion

"...the bright moon dropped..." – During the speaker's ride to Lucy's cottage, the moon has been setting.

SHE DWELT AMONG THE UNTRODDEN WAYS

springs of Dove – The Wordsworths lived in Dove cottage from December 1799 until May 1808. The "springs" can probably be found in the vicinity of this house in Grasmere.

I TRAVELLED AMONG UNKNOWN MEN

"Nor, England!...bore to thee." – This direct address to a non-living thing is known as an apostrophe.

"And thine too is the last green field..." – A similar sentiment is expressed in Wordsworth's *Intimations of Immortality* ode.

THREE YEARS SHE GREW IN SUN AND SHOWER

"And never more will be." – This sentiment of something gone forever is also expressed in many other Wordsworth poems, including his *Intimations of Immortality* ode.

A SLUMBER DID MY SPIRIT SEAL

—

ON THE CASTLE OF CHILLON

On the Castle of Chillon – This poem is another sonnet—14 lines of iambic pentameter, with a rhyme scheme of ABBA,ACCA,DEDEDE.

"...to fetters are consign'd..." – placed in chains, imprisoned

"And Freedom's fame finds wings on every wind." – Note the strong use of alliteration in this line.

Chillon – a castle in Geneva where a 16th-century Swiss patriot was imprisoned for resisting the French

Bonnivard – François Bonivard (c.1493–1570), the Swiss patriot imprisoned in Chillon

SHE WALKS IN BEAUTY

"She walks in beauty like the night..." – Notice the lack of end punctuation here; the lines read, "She walks in beauty like the night / of cloudless climes...," *not* simply as the phrase is usually quoted, "beauty like the night."

"Had half impaired..." – "Would have ruined"

raven tress – a lock of black hair

PROMETHEUS

Titan – In Greek mythology, the Titans were a race of giants; they represented the generation before the gods of Olympus. Prometheus, who was Zeus' uncle, was a Titan.

"The rock, the vulture, and the chain..." – Prometheus' punishment for stealing fire from the gods and giving it to humans was to be chained to a rock where a vulture would devour his liver every day. The liver would regenerate itself every night so the vulture could eat it again the next day.

Thunderer – a reference to Zeus, the god of thunder

"Thy Godlike crime was to be kind..." – The reason Prometheus stole fire for the human race was because all of the other gifts from the gods had been distributed to other animals.

OZYMANDIAS

Ozymandias – the Greek name for *Ramses*; the Ramses of this poem is probably the Egyptian pharaoh Ramses II, who is famous for his magnificent building projects. This poem is a sonnet—14 lines written in iambic pentameter with an odd rhyme scheme: ABAB, ACDC, EDE, FEF.

" 'My name is Ozymandias...and despair!' " – a wonderfully ambiguous statement that said to mighty rulers of the time that their works would never be able to rival Ozymandias' and to modern rulers that *all things* eventually decay and pass into oblivion. Note, however, that the enormous monument to the mighty ruler has itself become a ruin and a shadow of its former glory.

ODE TO THE WEST WIND

"O wild West Wind..." – Shelley begins the poem with an apostrophe. Pay attention to the manner in which Shelley rhymes the poem. The middle line of each short stanza is rhymed with the first and third lines of the next stanza. The rhyme scheme, therefore, is ABA, BCB, CDC, DED, EFE, etc.

fleeing, / Yellow – Notice the simile, comparing ghosts to falling leaves.

Mænad – a worshipper of Bacchus, in a frenzied religious ecstasy; the image here is that the clouds of the approaching storm resemble a wild-eyed woman, fingernails like claws, hair blowing madly in the wind, lips and chin stained with blood-red wine, who is running toward the speaker.

Baiae's bay – a popular ancient Roman resort at the western end of the Bay of Naples

ADONAIS

Adonais – This poem was written as an elegy for John Keats. The name *Adonais* is a combination of the Greek *Adonis,* a god concerned with fertility and the life/death/rebirth cycle, and *Adonai,* the Hebrew word for "Lord."

mighty Mother – another term for Aphrodite or Venus; she is the mother of Adonis. In Greek mythology, however, Urania was the lover of Adonis.

Urania – Aphrodite Urania, the daughter of Heaven (Uranus) and Light, representative of Heavenly love, intellectual aspiration, and abstract beauty

"He died" – This stanza is about the death of poet John Milton (1608–1674) who supported Parliament in the English Civil Wars of the 17th century. According to Shelley, Milton was the third of the great epic poets, the others being Homer and Dante. What Shelley is suggesting here is that Urania should not mourn the death of her son because Milton also died, and his spirit still reigns on Earth.

Sons of Light – the great epic poets, Homer, Dante, and Milton

"...youngest, dearest one has perished..." – a reference to Keats, who died at the age of 25

"To Phoebus was not Hyacinth so dear..." – Hyacinth was a Spartan prince beloved by the Greek god Phoebus Apollo. Apollo accidentally killed Hyacinth with a discus and made the flower, the hyacinth, from the boy's spilled blood.

Narcissus – a Greek youth who was so handsome that he fell in love with his own reflection

Albion – an ancient name for Great Britain or England

curse of Cain – an allusion to the biblical story of Cain and Abel; having slain his brother, Cain was banished from Eden and marked with a scar on his forehead. Anyone who killed Cain would be punished "sevenfold."

ambrosial – extremely pleasing to the taste and smell; the word comes from "ambrosia," the food the Greek gods ate, which gave them immortality.

"…obscene ravens…/…vultures…" – Ravens and vultures are scavengers that eat carrion.

Apollo – the Greek and Roman god of the sun, archery, and the arts

Pythian – Pythian Apollo, so named because he killed a python with his bow and arrow

Pilgrim of Eternity – a reference to Lord Byron

"…Ierne…lyrist of her saddest wrong…" – a reference to the Irish poet, Thomas Moore (1779–1852)

"one frail form…/…companionless…" – Shelley himself

Actaeon – a hunter who accidentally saw Diana, goddess of the hunt, bathing; angered at having been seen naked, Diana turned Actaeon into a stag, and he was pursued and torn to pieces by his own hounds.

Chatterton – Thomas Chatterton (1752–1770), an English poet who forged pseudo-medieval poetry; he committed suicide at the age of 17 and came to represent unacknowledged genius to the Romantics.

Sidney – possibly Algernon Sidney (1622–1683), who had supported Parliament in the English Civil Wars and was later executed for treason for involvement in a plot to once again abolish the monarchy and establish a republic in England

Lucan – Marcus Annaeus Lucanus (AD 39–65), a Roman poet sentenced to suicide for an alleged act of treason against the Emperor Nero

To Hope

—

Ode on Melancholy

Lethe – the river of forgetfulness, one of five rivers in the Greek underworld; the others are Acheron and Cocytus for woe and sorrow, Styx, which the gods would swear by, and Phlegethon, the river of fire.

Proserpine – Persephone, daughter of Ceres and wife of Hades

Psyche – the Greek notion of the soul; it is the root for the modern word *psychology*.

ODE TO A NIGHTINGALE

hemlock – a poisonous drink made from the hemlock, a shrub similar to a spruce, that was used in ancient Greece to carry out death sentences; Socrates committed suicide by drinking hemlock.

Lethe-wards – toward Lethe

Dryad – a female tree spirit in Greek mythology

Hippocrene – in Greek mythology, the name of a fountain on Mt. Helicon, sacred to the Muse; when drunk, the water was supposed to evoke poetic inspiration.

Bacchus – Dionysus, the Greek and Roman god of wine

Ruth – in the Old Testament, a widow who travels to a foreign land with her widowed mother-in-law; Ruth becomes the great-grandmother of King David.

Vocabulary

The Rime of the Ancient Mariner in Seven Parts

thence – from there

Part the First.
Eftsoons – soon afterwards; quickly
kirk – a church
ken – [Old English] see; know, understand
swound – a fainting spell
wherefore – why

Part the Second.
averred – asserted, insisted

Part the Third.
clombe – climbed
Gramercy! – an expression of gratitude
twain – the two crew members, male and female
weal – well-being
wist – to know, believe

Part the Fourth.
alway – always
hoar-frost – a light coating of frost or frozen dew
spectre-bark – a ghostly ship

Part the Fifth.
corses – corpses
nought – nothing
sere – withered, dry
silly – useless
wont – accustomed to

Part the Sixth.
perforce – by necessity
shrieve – variant form of *shrive*, to hear confession and offer absolution

Part the Seventh.
aught – anything
tod – a heavy mass
trow – to think, suppose

KUBLA KHAN OR A VISION IN A DREAM. A FRAGMENT.

athwart – crosswise

dulcimer – an instrument with taut strings that are plucked by the fingers, or struck with small padded hammers

sinuous – winding

THE LAMB: FROM *SONGS OF INNOCENCE*

mead – a meadow

THE TYGER: FROM *SONGS OF EXPERIENCE*

deeps – hidden places

THE CHIMNEY SWEEPER: FROM *SONGS OF INNOCENCE*

—

THE CHIMNEY SWEEPER: FROM *SONGS OF EXPERIENCE*

heath – open land full of low shrubs and flowers

A POISON TREE: FROM *SONGS OF EXPERIENCE*

sunnéd – nourished

wiles – trickery

LINES COMPOSED A FEW MILES ABOVE TINTERN ABBEY, ON REVISITING THE BANKS OF THE WYE DURING A TOUR, JULY 13, 1798 FROM *LYRICAL BALLADS*

burthen – a burden

cataract – a mountain waterfall

copses – small stands of trees

corporeal – having a physical body

interfused – blended in to become part of the very nature of something

roe – a young deer

sportive – playful

sylvan – similar to a park or wood

MY HEART LEAPS UP

—

ODE: *INTIMATIONS OF IMMORTALITY FROM RECOLLECTIONS OF EARLY CHILDHOOD*

apparelled – dressed

celestial – heavenly

cons – learns; studies carefully; memorizes

coronal – crowning

culling – picking, gathering

equipage – equipment, apparatus, furnishings
fugitive – quickly passing, short-lived
nurse – a governess, nanny
pipe – to play a flute, bagpipe, or other wind instrument
sallies – brief outbursts
tabor – a small drum
wheresoe'er – wherever

THE LUCY POEMS
STRANGE FITS OF PASSION HAVE I KNOWN
bent – traveled
boon – a benefit, favor, gift or act of kindness
cot – a cottage
lea – a pasture

SHE DWELT AMONG THE UNTRODDEN WAYS
untrodden – steps never taken

I TRAVELLED AMONG UNKNOWN MEN
bowers – arbors; shelters made of vines and tree branches woven together
wheel – a spinning wheel

THREE YEARS SHE GREW IN SUN AND SHOWER
balm – a soothing ointment
dell – a small valley
glade – a grassy open space in a forest
heath – a marshy, overgrown wasteland
insensate – inanimate; without sensation or feeling
kindle – to begin to glow
rivulets – tiny streams, usually of rain water

A SLUMBER DID MY SPIRIT SEAL
diurnal – daily; occuring every day

ON THE CASTLE OF CHILLON
habitation – where one lives

SHE WALKS IN BEAUTY
aspect – bearing, composure, demeanor
climes – climates
gaudy – tastelessly over-decorated

PROMETHEUS
funereal – mournful, somber
inexorable – inflexible, unyielding
recompense – payment

OZYMANDIAS
visage – the face; facial features

ODE TO THE WEST WIND
azure – blue in color
clarion – an advance announcement
cleave – to cut, separate
dirge – a funeral song
impetuous – forceful, violent; impulsive
lyre – a stringed musical instrument similar to a small harp
pumice – a light, porous stone
sepulchre – [sepulcher] a tomb
zenith – the highest point; the point in the sky; directly overhead

ADONAIS
alit – landed, settled
anadem – a wreath for the head
bier – a stand on which a corpse or coffin is placed for a public funeral
brere – [archaic] briar, a thorny plant
calumny – slander
carrion kites – scavenger birds
chastisement – a reprimand or punishment
compeer – a peer; a person who is on equal standing with another in a group
draught – a draft; a long drink
dross – worthless waste material
effluence – outflow
ensanguined – covered or stained, as with blood
firmament – the sky or heaven
girt – encircled as with a belt or girdle
incarnation – having life in human or physical form
knell – the tolling of funeral bells
liberticide – a killer of liberty
lorn – left or abandoned
mien – an appearance or bearing, especially as it reveals mood or personality
moulder – to disintegrate; turn to dust
pard-like – resembling a leopard
pendulous – wavering, indecisive

Phantasies – fantastic dreams
plastic – giving form or shape to a substance
ruth – compassion for another's misery; sorrow, pity
sate – sat
satiate – to satisfy
superincumbent – lying on top of; smothering
viperous – like a snake, venomous; malicious

TO HOPE

bequest – a legacy
ethereal – heavenly; intangible, having no physical substance
pinions – wings, feathers

ODE ON MELANCHOLY

palate – the roof of the mouth; sense of good taste
rosary of yew-berries – prayer beads made of poisonous berries
nightshade – a poisonous mushroom
sovran – a sovereign
Wolf's-bane – a type of poisonous plant

ODE TO A NIGHTINGALE

casements – windows
darkling – enclosed in darkness
eglantine – a kind of rose, sweetbriar
fays – fairies
pards – leopards
plaintive – sad, mournful
poesy – poetry
requiem – a funeral mass or a hymn for the dead
verdurous – green, lush vegetation